MILD ALE

The Classic Beer Style Series is devoted to offering in-depth information on world-class styles by exploring their history, flavor profiles, brewing methods, recipes, and ingredients.

OTHER BOOKS IN THE CLASSIC BEER STYLE SERIES

MILD ALE

History, Brewing Techniques, Recipes

David Sutula

Classic Beer Style
Series No. 15

brewers
publications

A Division of the
Association of Brewers
Boulder, Colorado

Brewers Publications, Division of the Association of Brewers
PO Box 1679, Boulder, CO 80306-1679
(303) 447-0816; Fax (303) 447-2825

Direct all inquiries to the above address.

Printed in the United States of America
10 9 8 7 6 5 4

ISBN-13: 978-0-937381-68-7

Unless otherwise noted, all interior photographs are by Shelley Sutula. All labels and coasters courtesy of Brian Glover.

Permission for use of the following items on the cover photo is gratefully acknowledged: Avery Brewing Company for the use of their midland Mild beer and It's Your Move gaming store in Boulder, Colorado for the use of the dominoes.

Library of Congress Cataloging-in-Publication Data
Sutula, David.
     Mild ale : history, brewing techniques, recipes / David Sutula.
        p.   cm. — (Classic beer style series ; 15)
     Includes bibliographical references and index.
     ISBN 0-937381-68-3 (alk. paper)
     1. Ale. I. Title. II. Series.
TP578.S88   1999
641.8'73—dc21   98-43604
                                                        CIP

In loving memory of my dad, Ted Sutula,
who taught me that "wherever you go, there you are."

Contents

Contents

Acknowledgments

No book can get off the ground, much less get published, without the benefit of an intricate support network. At the helm of my personal network are my wife, Shelley, my daughters, Abbey and Kaitlyn, and my parents, Ted and Marilyn (Sutulas all). They have always supported my writing, even though it has often entailed long hours at my desk on evenings and weekends when I should have been cutting the grass or finishing the deck I started two years ago.

Next, I have to mention my brewing colleagues—Brian O'Reilly of John Harvard's Brew House in Cleveland and Bill Bryson of Wallaby's Brewpub and Grille in Westlake—to whom I owe little thanks. Had they not led me astray with promises of beer and merriment, this volume might have been completed far sooner than it was. Seriously, though, they read the manuscript and offered a lot of great advice and comment that has improved the book.

Then there are the people within the local brewing community who are always ready to tackle a technical question, offer sound advice on the basis of long years of experience, and tell me that I've lost my mind when I come up with a half-baked theory. Thanks go to Tim

Rastetter of Liberty Street Brewing Company, Dan Maerzluft, formerly of Diamondback Brewing Company, Andy Craze and Damon Smith of Western Reserve Brewing Company, Andy Tveekrem and Rob Garrity of Great Lakes Brewing, Brad Unruh of Four Fellows Brewpub, Stephen Danckers of Crooked River Brewing Company, and almost every other member of the Northern Ohio Craft Brewer's Association (NOCBA).

I must also thank many of the people in the extended brewing community, including Tim Morse, Emperor of Brewing Operations for John Harvard's, who encouraged this project even though I threatened to turn one of his breweries into a mild-only facility. Bill Morgan of Nippon Brewery in Japan and John Mallett of Saaz Brewing Services in Arlington, Virginia, offered free advice whenever I called and never sent me an invoice for consultation (I hope this grateful acknowledgment will not serve as a reminder). Ray Daniels of the Craft Beer Institute in Chicago lent a great deal of time and energy that could have been spent putting together the Real Ale Festival; he willingly answered my questions, allowed me to pick his brain, and helped me source some of the more esoteric references in the history section.

William Crisp, of Crisp Malting, and Brian Glover of Cardiff, Wales, are to be thanked for loaning me some original prose and artwork for use in this volume. And last, but not least, a huge thanks goes to Roger Protz of the Campaign for Real Ale in the United Kingdom, for doing some legwork overseas and debating the "mild ale versus brown ale" conundrum with me.

Finally, there are the guys I started my brewing hobby/career with. I'm grateful for the support I received from Brad Priebe, my good friend, with whom I made some of my first homebrew; John and Jim Pastor of the Grape and Granary (easily the best homebrew shop in the northern hemisphere); Ken Bowmer and Dan Siko of the Dirt Floor Brewing Company; Mark Ward, with whom I've shared the best beers in the world (some of which he brewed); Fred Karm of the Thirsty Dog Brewing Company, and all the members of the Society of Northern Ohio Brewers (SNOBS) and the Society of Akron Area Zymurgists (SAAZ).

I would also like to extend a heartfelt thanks to one of the best people I've ever had the privilege of knowing: Scott Eatmon, my fraternity brother and the best damn bartender from Timbuktu to Portland, Oregon. Scott gave up a substantial portion of his vacation and never complained as I dragged him from brewery to brewery throughout England, Ireland, and Scotland (not to mention Bontfein, Wales).

Introduction

It was during my first years as a homebrewer that I was introduced to the mild ale style. I had recently graduated to all-grain brewing after only a handful of extract and minimash attempts and was on a quest for the perfect pint of porter. I had fallen in love with a local example—Great Lakes Edmund Fitzgerald Porter—that at the time was not being bottled and was available only at the pub; it has since become a classic. I knew that porter was supposed to be dark and full of flavor, but I had absolutely no experience in formulation. I had been working with the only hop that I knew existed—Cascade.

My first all-grain attempt was a complete disaster. The beer was problematic on a huge scale. In retrospect, I believe I had mashed at too high a temperature, receiving a very low extract from the grains. But I would not have been able to verify this even had I known what the proper temperature and gravity should have been, as I owned neither a thermometer nor a hydrometer. In the end, what little extract I did get was horribly infected and smelled of old sneakers and wet dog.

This failed attempt led me to a local homebrewing shop, the Grape and Granary, in Akron, Ohio, where I bought a thermometer and a new set of brewing supplies. Sensing my desire to brew great beer and the limitations of my budget, shop owners Jim and John Pastor gave me my first hydrometer. I left with my new instruments and one more useful piece of the puzzle—my porter should have a gravity of about 1.060 on the hydrometer.

Because I was still paying far too little attention to the details of my brewing practices, my second attempt at brewing a porter came out a little thin (on the shallow side of 1.035) but tasty. It may have been intuition, direct intervention by the beer gods, or just a damn lucky guess, but I decided to lower my hopping rate proportionately to the lower gravity. The resulting beer still had a definite spiciness imparted by the Cascade hops, but it was nicely balanced by the chocolate and crystal malts I had used.

Although I could not call it a porter, I was nonetheless proud of the beer and brought a few bottles to a friend's house. I was certain that he would tell me that I'd botched the job and encourage me to find a new calling. (I've always needed a bit of discouragement to solidify my goals.) My friend Ken Bowmer had lived in England for most of his life and had taken up the hobby of brewing there several years before moving to the United States.

Ken popped open one of my brews and poured it into the familiar dimpled glass from which I had seen him sampling his own brews. He smelled the beer and, after pausing to think a moment, took a hefty slug and swished it around his mouth before swallowing. After another moment of contemplation he spoke: "If you were to walk into a pub in Stourbridge and ask for a pint of dark mild, this is what you would get." He must have mistook the puzzled expression on my face as one of pride because he was quick to qualify his comment. "Except for the Cascades. *If this beer had been made with a proper English hop, it would be perfect*," he said.

At the time, I thought I was a very clever fellow because I had written down exactly what I had done to get that beer to taste the way it did. (I did not yet realize that any brewer worth his salt keeps meticulous records.) I went back to the homebrew shop and picked up an identical set of supplies, except for two small changes: This time, John suggested Fuggle as a "proper English hop" and set me up with a gold-foil packet of liquid yeast. I set about the task of re-creating the beer. Eleven hours of work, eleven days of waiting and worrying, and . . . success! Ken pronounced this beer the perfect dark mild.

So, now I faced the big question—what was a dark mild? Was there such a thing as a pale mild? light mild? For help, I turned to Ken. He said a mild was a low-alcohol beer that several breweries in the Midlands of England make.

Ken knew a good mild—that was for sure—but he had a little trouble coming up with the information I needed, so I turned to Charlie Papazian. He wrote that "mild is a brown ale of low-alcohol strength . . . not particularly robust or hoppy. . . . A small amount of black patent or chocolate malt adds color more than flavor. . . . Milds are quick to mature and easy to duplicate authentically."[1]

Besides being a little lean on the hard facts about mild ale, Papazian's summation was not what I wanted to hear. My beer, while not an intense flavor experience, was certainly robust. The chocolate malt I added had definitely had an impact on its flavor. To be honest, what hurt my ego the most was the little comment about how easy milds were to make.

The next source I looked to was Roger Protz. He maintains that mild ales are simply the draught version of brown ale.[2] That just didn't seem right. It was too simple—and if it were true, why would Protz dedicate a whole chapter, separate from brown ale, to milds?

Now more confused than enlightened, I finally turned to Michael Jackson. He wrote, "porter's sweeter, gentler young brother, mild was originally a London style. . . . It should be low in hop bitterness (which is what mild means). . . . Although a mild is not necessarily very attenuated, its low gravity makes for a modest calorie count."[3] Although still a little weak on "news I could use," Jackson's account did tell me that there are both pale (also known as light) and dark milds, that there are still a good number of them being made, and that the style is suffering from declining sales— even vanishing in some areas.

The general lack of information available about the style caused my interest to fade nearly as quickly as that second batch of mild disappeared from my cellar. Once the beer was gone, I was back full-time on my quest for porter. Since it seemed from the little research I had done that mild was somehow connected both to porter and to brown ale, I thought I might be able to learn more about mild as I pursued the other two styles. I never found the perfect pint of porter. I learned that there were far too many diverse and equally fulfilling interpretations of the style to ever pronounce one the quintessential pint.

It was not until several years later, after turning my passion for beer into a profession in brewing, when I was sitting in a pub in a small village called Himley outside

Dudley in the English West Midlands, that I had a flash-back to that bottle of homebrew I had shared with Ken Bowmer. I had ordered half a pint of Highgate Dark Mild, which the landlord had informed me was made only a few miles up the road in Walsall. With one sip, I knew that Ken had been right—my porter-gone-awry had been an accidental mild ale success.

I questioned the landlord about the beer. He knew of only a few other examples being produced, and most of them were being made within a few miles of his pub. He said that milds were the "elixir of life for the salt of the Earth." Milds are low-alcohol beers with plenty of flavor and body, he said. They were dwindling in number very quickly, and had it not been for the coal mining folk of the Black Country, they might have died out entirely years ago.

That half pint (and the subsequent two full pints) of Highgate Mild renewed my interest in the style and, armed with my *1995 CAMRA Good Beer Guide*, I set out on another quest. (CAMRA is the Campaign for Real Ale, a consumer rights group formed in the United Kingdom that advocates the brewing of real ales.) This time I was not in search of the perfect pint—I was in search of the style as a whole. I had to know what mild was about.

Where did it come from, and where was it going? Why was the style dying, and what could be done to save it? What could *I* do to save it? What did the style do for the people of the Black Country who loved it so, and what could the style do for Americans? How could I bring it, as well as an appreciation for mild, back to my brewery halfway around the globe?

What I found was that mild is a link to the past—a living relic from the roots of the English brewing industry. It has existed for at least 300 years, and its past is inexorably entwined with the histories of porter, stout, brown ale, and every other English ale. It is a beer that embodies the genteel spirit and hearty culture of the people who have brewed it and those who drink it. It is a restorative, an aperitif, and a session beer. Mild assumes every role that a beverage can, somehow transforming itself to fit the moment and the occasion.

Unfortunately, mild is at the same crossroad that its cousin, porter, reached in the early 1970s—at the threshold of extinction. So, on to the second part of my resolution—to do what I can to save mild as a style. The problems with mild, or so I thought at the time, were twofold: it was only a sub-style of brown ale, and there were very few original resources regarding the history and practice of brewing mild. As it turned out, I was wrong on both counts. There is a clear case for mild being a style on its own, and there are hundreds of references to it in the canon of brewing literature.

This book is not meant to be the last word on mild ale. As you will discover, the great thing about the style is that it offers unparalleled flexibility and potential for varied interpretation. Therefore, only the brewer and the brewer's customers can truly have the last say. This book is merely a starting point—an outline of the historical development, past forms, and modern-day identity of the mild ale style.

I hope that after reading this book, you will be as convinced as I am that mild is a style worth saving. Too many brewers are dropping mild from their product lines or dropping the *mild* moniker in favor of less-meaningful terms like *dark* or *light bitter*. How can the significance—even the identity—of such a historically important beer style be lost to modern minds? The question defies easy answers. It is, however, my ardent hope that mild will find new life, just as other beers such as porter and stout are enjoying revivalist success.

An increasing number of American craftbrewers are now experimenting with milds, and there are indications that traditional mild is making something of a comeback on its native soil as well. With renewed interest in the art, science, and business of small-scale brewing in the United States and Europe—as well as in markets as far flung as Thailand, New Zealand, Costa Rica, and China—it seems likely that mild ale will continue to enjoy a proud position in the line-up of classic beer styles for years to come.

CHAPTER 1

Mild Ale: The Historical Perspective

Mild ale is one of the least-known and least-appreciated styles today. Unlike other declining styles that have been rediscovered in the craftbrewing revival of recent times, mild ale is continuing to lose market share. Brewers who still offer a mild ale in their product line ask themselves almost every day whether it is worth it. The reasons behind the rise and fall of mild ale's popularity are more obscure than the causes of waning popularity for its better-known brethren.

Mild ale had its roots in a time when most brewing was done by private citizens for their own use or by publicans for the use of a small number of patrons. The terms *mild*, *old*, and *stock* are among the oldest words used to describe British beer. Any discussion of the history of brewing the style we know today as mild ale must necessarily begin with an overview of the history of brewing in Britain. The origins of mild ale are inextricably entwined with the histories of brown ale, porter, old ale, and every other style of traditional British ale.

The Roots of Brewing in Britain

The Roman technical and scientific writer Pliny the Younger (circa 61–113 A.D.) noted that the Britannic Celts brewed a beverage they called *curmi*. Ignoring the hops that most likely grew wild throughout the forests of Britain, the Celts seasoned their curmi with other plants, such as rosemary, yarrow, and bog myrtle.[1]

When the Angles, Saxons, Jutes, and Danes invaded and settled England in the fifth and sixth centuries, they brought with them a tremendous thirst for beer, as well as their native language. Their word for malt liquor was *öl*, which is the root for the modern word *ale*. Back then (and for centuries to come), the word referred to a beverage made with malted grains, but without the benefit of hops.

In the first century A.D., the Romans brought plenty of wine along when they invaded Britain. When that bounty ran out, soldiers frustrated by supply lines that were long and hard to maintain in that northernmost outpost of civilization began to manufacture and consume what was viewed by most as a thoroughly uncivilized drink. The Emperor Julian's disdain for beer was evident when he wrote that this "wine made from barley" smelled of goat.[2]

Nevertheless, the Roman legions soon developed a taste for beer. A recent excavation near the Black Lion pub on Fishpool Street in St. Albans, Hertfordshire, revealed ancient floor maltings built by the Romans that no doubt supplied brewers in the nearby town of Verulamium. Although the Romans ate steamed hop shoots as a delicacy, they did not use the plant in their brewing process.[3]

English Brewing 1066–1720: A Cottage Industry

When the Normans invaded Britain in 1066, they found that the Anglo-Saxons had developed a very healthy brewing industry. The *Domesday Book*, a vast ledger compiled by the Normans to catalog everything in England for taxation purposes, lists numerous private breweries and specifies the standards by which they were to be taxed. Although the infant brewing industry was sufficiently organized enough to come under the scrutiny of the taxman, brewing methods were still relatively unsophisticated. It was a "catch-as-catch-can" process; brewers used methods handed down from generation to generation, making modifications as they saw fit. Little regard was given to matters of sanitation or science, as neither was understood by even the scholars of the time—much less by the common people.

The raw materials available to these early brewers were often of low and inconsistent quality. The brewing water was frequently infected or laced with undesirable trace elements. The only analytical method available, other than tasting the water to check its flavor, was a simple hardness test. If the brewer could easily bring a small quantity of soap to a thick lather, the water was soft; if not, the water was hard.[4]

The nuances of genetic selection were unknown, so the malted barley used to produce these early beers would have been made from locally grown varieties that had been domesticated from the available wild stock. It is likely that the disease-resistance and yield of these crops would have been poor and the malting process poorer yet. The simplest malting method still in use has been briefly described by Michael Jackson, who has seen farmer-brewers in Norway germinate their barley by tying a sack of unmalted barley corns to a rock in a swiftly flowing stream.[5] Alternatively, the malt may have been sprouted on the stone floors of farm outbuildings. This is almost certainly how the barley in the first beers was malted, and simple methods like these were part of the malting process until the sixteenth century. In fact, poor drainage and a lack of control over the environment, coupled with general ignorance of the mechanisms behind the malting process, probably resulted in poorly modified barley until the seventeenth century.

Kilning was another problem. The wood fires used for kilning rendered a significant proportion of the malt useless due to charring and burning, in addition to giving a pronounced smoky character to the grain and the ale. Curing the malt over wood fires or over burning straw and peat was an inexact and uncontrollable method. No malt lighter than nut brown could be produced because the intense heat caramelized the outside of the kernels. Attempts to roast malt to darker colors would have caused a chain melanoidin reaction that would have turned the malt into charcoal.[6] With the possible exceptions of sun-drying malts and kilning over low-intensity straw fires to produce lighter colored malts, there would have been very little variation in the color of ales—the vast majority were brown.

One of the earliest references to a product known as mild ale comes from a rental agreement recorded sometime in the late twelfth century. Ceolred Abbot of

Medeshamstede (modern-day Peterborough), Wales, charged his tenant, Wulfred, 1 horse, 30 shillings, 15 mittan of clear ale, 5 mittan of Welsh ale, and 15 sesters of mild ale for a one-year lease to an estate at Sempringham.[7] We cannot be sure what the clear ale was, although it is logical to assume that it was a strong product made of malted barley, with no seasonings whatsoever, that had been aged in wooden containers. The Welsh ale would have been a heavy, pre-Norman, pre-Saxon drink laced with expensive spices and often sweetened with honey. The mild ale of twelfth-century Britain was simply an ale—either strong or relatively weak—that was intended for present use and did not exhibit the earthy, woody roundness that is imparted by a secondary fermentation involving the wild yeast *Brettanomyces*. This character, along with a lactic acid sourness from the action of lactobacillus and other acid-producing microbes, were the hallmarks of the older, aged stock or stale ales and were almost certainly a facet of both the clear ale and the Welsh ale Coelred was referring to.

Between the eleventh and eighteenth centuries, the prevailing brewing method was a system known as parti-gyle brewing, in which three or more successively weaker worts were drawn from a single mash. The brewing equipment or utensils used were primitive and unsanitary. Often made solely of wood, they teemed with wild yeasts and bacteria, both of which would have had a profound effect on the beer. In fact, beer so spoiled as to be unfit for use must have been common-place, as wooden vessels did not lend themselves to boiling or other methods of cleaning.

When a metal kettle (later called a copper) was used, it was

A primitive mash tub.

almost certainly accompanied by wooden mash tuns, fermentation tuns, and, worst of all in terms of sanitation, cool-ships—large, shallow wooden vessels in which the unfermented wort was allowed to sit, exposed to the air and the wood, while cooling to a pitchable temperature. The mash tun was the most specialized of the brewing utensils, yet it was usually little more than a large container with a tap fixed near the bottom.

The brewer's art was based upon empirical observation and traditional methods. For the first gyle, a quantity of water was raised to a boil and then allowed to cool until the steam escaping had subsided and the surface of the water turned from a turbid shimmer to a reflective and glasslike calm.[8] The brewers knew that this was the temperature at which they could gain the

A small brew house, circa 1747. Notice the empty wooden casks that were used as fermenters. The beer would later go to the market in these same casks.

most value from their grain. The grains were stirred into the hot water, and the resulting mash was left to stand for some time. After the concoction turned sweet to the taste, the stick or plug jammed into the hole at the bottom of the mash tun was knocked out, and the sweet liquid was run off, with little regard given to clarity or to anything else.

The wort was then transferred to a boiling vessel, which might or might not have been made of wood, and boiled by any means the brewer could manage. This may have been accomplished by heating stones (or, later, pieces of iron, bronze, or other metals) and dropping them into the liquid, or by placing superheated coals underneath the tun. Boils conducted in one of these imprecise ways would necessarily be weak and under-productive.

The second gyle would be started as soon as the first was out of the mash vessel. More water would be brought to temperature and mixed with the grains left from the first gyle. As before, the valve would be opened (or the plug removed) and the liquid would then be boiled. Each successive wort drawn from the grain would be lower in specific gravity, producing a beer that was weaker in alcoholic strength.

The first gyle, being the strongest wort, was fermented and stored in wooden vats or barrels where it could mellow and age. Beers resulting from this first gyle were known as old, stale, or stock ales. The second gyle produced a beer still high in alcohol, but less-suited to long aging in a wooden container; it was usually blended with the old or stock ales.

The most common ales of the Norman period were undoubtedly of the stale or stock variety blended with a portion of the beer produced from the middle and subsequent gyles. In addition to being brewed and fermented in wood containers, these stock or stale beers underwent a substantial aging period in wooden casks. There, the harshness of the spices used and the smokiness of the malt would mellow as the beer picked up the hallmark "horsey" aroma and flavor of a wild-yeast fermentation. Despite the long aging period, stock beers were still harsh, and they benefited from being blended with the beer from the weaker gyles.

Because refrigeration was unknown and because the role of yeast and other microflora in the fermentation and spoilage of beer was not understood, brewing was a seasonal activity that typically took place in the cooler months of the year. A very high alcoholic content was needed to prevent airborne microorganisms—and those colonizing the porous wood of the brewing utensils—from rendering these beers unfit for consumption after long periods of storage during the summer months.

The last and weakest gyle produced a beer with a much lower alcohol content. Those beers were known as small, table, or family beers. Although the last gyle was certainly the weakest of the lot, the strength of those family beers was considerable. They would make today's strong and old ales pale by comparison.

Although big beers by today's standards, the beers from the third gyle—and in some cases even fourth or fifth gyles—lacked the sugars to produce ales of sufficient strength to keep for very long. These beers, called small, present-use, or running beers among other things, were meant to be consumed as quickly as possible, before the infectious organisms had time to run wild and turn the ale into vinegar. The present-use ales were undoubtedly harsh with the flavor of green apples and perhaps turbid with yeast cells and microbes when first tapped, and they must have turned sour and acidic just before they were run out. Even so, they were the first mild ales.

Sometimes the three different worts were treated as separate products and left to ferment on their own. Other times they were mixed, either all together or in a specified combination with one or more other worts to produce the desired effects. Mixing the three products from separate casks at the publican's house immediately before serving customers was a popular practice in Britain until the early nineteenth century.[9] The resulting product, sometimes called three-threads, is believed to have spurred the development of porter. Until very recent times, the practice survived in a few pubs in Ireland, where customers were offered a strong, well-aged beer mixed with weaker, fresh beers from two different casks.[10]

Mild in Popular Literature:
An Early Reference

The theory that mild ale was, at first, used to designate the beers made from the lower-gravity runnings and served relatively young (as opposed to the higher-gravity "old" beers) is evidenced by this excerpt from a sixteenth-century poetic epic. Note that the phrase "new and old" in the chorus replaces "mild and old" in the refrains.

I can eat but little meat,
My stomach is not good;
But sure I think that I can drink
    With him that wears a hood.
Though I go bare, take ye no care
    I am nothing a cold,
I stuff my skin so full within
    Of jolly good mild and old.

Back and side go bare, go bare,
Both foot and hand go cold;
But, belly, God send thee good ale enough,
Whether it be new or old.

I have no roast but a nut-brown toast,
    And a crab laid in the fire;
A little bread shall do me stead—
    Much bread I not desire.
No frost, no snow, no wind I trow,
    Can hurt me if I wold,

> *I and so wrapt and thoroughly lapt*
> > *Of jolly good mild and old.*
>
> *Back and side go bare, go bare,*
> *Both foot and hand go cold;*
> *But, belly, God send thee good ale enough,*
> *Whether it be new or old.*
>
> *And Tib, my wife. That is her life*
> > *Loveth well good ale to seek,*
> *Full oft drinks she, till ye may see*
> > *The tear run down her cheek;*
> *Then doth she troll me to the bowl,*
> > *Even as a malt-worm should,*
> *And saith "Sweetheart, I took my part*
> > *Of this jolly good mild and old."*
>
> *Back and side go bare, go bare,*
> *Both foot and hand go cold;*
> *But, belly, God send thee good ale enough,*
> *Whether it be new or old.*
>
> —William Still, Bishop of
> Bath and Wells, 1566

The term *mild*, then, was used to designate a whole class of beers rather than a distinct and separate style throughout the seventeenth and eighteenth centuries and even into the nineteenth century. It is therefore likely that most seventeenth- and eighteenth-century beers existed in both a stock (or stale) form and in a mild form, and that both stock and mild ales could be found in a wide range, albeit a high range, of gravities. Prior to the advent of porter brewing, beers were classified not by their color, flavor, or other attributes, but rather by their age and by the methods with which they were brewed and conditioned.

It is at this point—before 1720— that all of the traditional English styles of beer have become intertwined, and it is from this point that they all diverge. It was difficult to draw a distinct line between the various styles offered prior to 1720, much as it is difficult to define the differences between many stouts and porters today. Three-threads, it is believed, gave rise to porter. And when porter hit the market in the 1720s, the usefulness of the other styles as components in a mixture was outlived, but they found a strong following on their own.

Hops—and, by extension, the term *bier* or *beer*— did not come into use until the middle of the sixteenth century.[11] Hops were first used for brewing in England after Dutch traders brought cultivated strains of the plant to Kent and Sussex, along with examples of the Germanic beer brewed with it. It was at this time that English brewers began to use the hop to spice their ales, using relatively little of the spice and often in conjunction with other spices. They used a larger quantity of hops for a stronger beer.[12] Today, some British revivalist brewers are experimenting with herbs like anise and ginger in their brews; some Nordic and Baltic brewers never abandoned the old methods, and they regularly use spices like juniper and bog myrtle.[13]

Beer—that is, malt liquor spiced with hops—did not replace the traditional unhopped ale right away. Because hops were brought by traders and were mainly available to people with easy access to the marketplace, brewing with hops became popular in the cities, but the traditional methods were still commonplace in the country.

Writing in 1868 about the merits of hops as a preservative in beer, George Stewart Amsinck tells us that he had "tasted Ale brewed in Devonshire, a twelve-month old, with only 6 lbs. per quarter, perfectly sound, in fact mild, and on the other hand, I have met with East India Pale, from one of the largest Breweries in Burton, with 30 lbs. to the quarter, at the end of the month of August quite sour." Amsinck confirms that beers that did not exhibit the lactic sourness common to beers aged for many months were called mild. (For the record, Amsinck was refuting the then-popular belief that hops had a latent preservative effect on beer. This has since been proven to be true, but Amsinck was far from convinced.)

In the late seventeenth and early eighteenth centuries, English country brewers began producing and selling pale beers. To distinguish their products from those of the competition, London brewers used the term *brown beer* to describe their products, which seem to have included porter, stout, brown, and all types of darker beers in both their stock and mild forms. One of the earliest references to a product called brown ale is in *The London and Country Brewer* from 1750, and the *Private Brewer's Guide* of 1822 says that "the consumption of brown beer became confined to London . . . a mixture of stale, mild and pale, which was called three threads . . . Being the beverage of laboring men, . . . it obtained the name porter, and was called intire [sic] butt beer."[14] It is clear that *brown beer* was not

Boddingtons is one of many U.K. breweries that calls the bottled version of their mild ale a "brown ale."

used to designate a particular and distinct style of beer, but rather to identify any beer that was not of the new pale variety.

Mild Ale's Cousins: Porter and Stout

> *I sing, I sing of good times older,*
> *When men than women were the bolder;*
> *When bills were short and credit shorter,*
> *And when from malt they brew'd the porter;*
> *When lawyers were too proud to pillage,*
> *And Horselydown was but a village;*
> *Christmas had its Christmas carols,*
> *And ladies' sides were hoop'd like barrels;*
> *When drinking ale made men stronger,*
> *And doctors made folks live longer;*
> *When our grand-dads brew'd the stout October;*
> *And thought it a sin to go to bed sober.*
>
> Chorus
> *Sing hey, sing ho! I can but grieve*
> *for the good old days of Adam and Eve.*
> —Eighteenth-century song

The origins of brewing as an art and practical means of producing a potable beverage are obscured by the mists of time, but the date at which brewing ceased to be a cottage industry and became a technological industry is easily pinpointed. The story goes that one afternoon in the autumn of 1722, a partner in the Bell Brewhouse in Shoreditch, an entrepreneurial chap named Ralph Harwood, grew tired of delivering three separate casks to each of his publicans so that they could mix them in the customer's tankard as three-threads. Harwood's solution was to brew a beer that exhibited all the characteristics of three-threads but could be served from a single cask. The new beer was called entire butt or intire, as it was a single beer that could be served "as is" from one cask or butt.

This new dark, nourishing, thick, and bitter beer found favor with porters and other manual workers who were attracted to it because of its greater apparent strength.[15] There are several variations of this story, which first appeared in *The Curiosities of Ale and Beer* by John Bickerdyke, but what is certain is that porter brewing, and by extension stout brewing, eventually pushed the brewing industry into the modern era.

It is probable that Harwood's achievement, while very romantic, was only a small part of the real story. During this time, when the technical advantages of thermometers and hydrometers were not yet available, brewers were reluctant to share their secrets with competitors. An achievement the magnitude of Harwood's would surely have been worth keeping secret. But beginning in 1726, a product called "porter" is referred to in many sources. This seems to indicate that just four years after Harwood invented it, porter had become a widely produced style.

If one were inclined to believe that Harwood was simply a beer philanthropist who divulged his secret in a selfless campaign for the advancement of the industry, he must have surely been a martyr as well, because at no time is Harwood mentioned as a leading porter brewer. By 1758, he was only brewing about 21,000 barrels of porter a year, while the leading enterprises—including the future industry giant, Whitbread—were producing between 55,000 and 65,000 barrels. Just two years later, he did not even produce enough to be included in the published list of important brewers.[16]

What is more likely is that Harwood was one of the first to produce a single-gyle beer—a beer that was designed to withstand maturation and to be pleasing to the palate as served from a single barrel. All of Harwood's blending was done at the brewery, in much the same manner as modern large breweries blend their beers to be consistent in terms of flavor and appearance.

This was a very important development because the mild ale producers of the time almost certainly followed suit, designing single-gyle beers to resemble the popular parti-gyle products they formerly produced. For the first time, lines could be drawn between distinct styles of beer.

Technological Innovation

Porter brewing gave rise to a whole new set of problems. In the years immediately before the advent of porter, the brewing trade mainly produced mild ales. These ales were formidable in strength by today's standards, 1.070 to 1.080 specific gravity (SG), but they were not as strong as the new porters. Consequently, the milds could be brewed, fermented, and aged in the trade barrels—the casks or butts in which they would be carried to market in about a month and a half. Porter and other strong beers had to be aged in the casks for up to a year or more. In 1743, Robert Huck's brewery, Thrale's and Truman's, owned several thousand butts each (1 butt = 108 imperial gallons).[17] Because of the enormous storage capacity required, brewers had to store their butts in every conceivable nook and cranny. When there was no more room

The porter vats at Barclay and Perkins in London, circa 1850. The brewery had well over 100 vats that held from 500 to 4,000 barrels each.

on their premises, they were forced to incur the added expense of renting space elsewhere. In addition, they bore the considerable expense of repairing and replacing the butts, which typically lasted no more than 15 years.[18]

The first innovation spawned by consumer demand for porter was the installation of vats for aging instead of trade barrels. Parson's Brewery in London's South End was the innovator behind this advancement. Great oaken vats that could hold 1,500 barrels each were constructed there in 1736; those same vats were still in use as late as 1774. The vats cost far less per barrel of beer and quickly became a source of pride and point of competition between neighboring brewers. By 1784, the newest Whitbread cisterns held 2,400 barrels of beer; one hundred people dined inside one of Thrale's new vats in the year 1800, and in 1809, one vat at the Golden Lane Brewery held 7,000 barrels.

All of this one-upsmanship finally led to disaster on the evening of October 17, 1814. A vat at Meaux's Horse Shoe Brewery in St. Giles containing 7,600 barrels of porter burst, washing away the brewery walls, crushing buildings across the street, and flooding basements all along Bainbridge Street. Eight people died of "drowning, injury, poisoning by the porter fumes or drunkeness."[19]

Other innovations also had sweeping effects on the brewing industry. Since the late sixteenth century, maltsters had been experimenting with coal-fired kilns and indirect curing of the malt, giving rise to the first pale malts. These new malts were very expensive because coal was difficult to mine at first, and it produced huge amounts of soot and noxious fumes when it burned. Not until the late seventeenth century did the less-costly coke become readily available. At the same time these new fuels became popular, brewers were increasingly interested in selecting hop cultivars for their flavor and bittering properties; they also had gained a better understanding of the role of water hardness in brewing. All of these factors came together to boost the production of pale ales—the beers that would eventually dominate the British beer market and claim the lion's share of the market for mild ale.

In 1817, David Wheeler invented the cylindrical drum roaster. Grain (or beans, as in the case of coffee) could be roasted while water was added in small amounts to control the process.[20] This patented process allowed the maltster or brewer more control over the curing of his malt, making it possible to produce a broad spectrum of malt colors—and flavors—more easily and more consistently than in the past. The still-popular black patent malt traces the origin of its name to Wheeler's patented process.

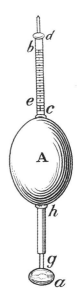

An early hydrometer.

Two more great innovations in British brewing were made in the late eighteenth century by James Baverstock, who experimented with the hydrometer, and by John Richardson, who devised a method of calculating the extract potential of a given sample of malt. Their findings led to the decline of brown malt. Brewers discovered that they could expect more yield per pound of malt with the pale varieties than with the brown varieties. Cost per pound was no longer the determining factor—cost per percent sugar revealed that pale malt was the cheaper way to go.

These discoveries had the greatest impact on the porter breweries. Until this time, porter had been made exclusively of brown malt. But with the new malts and confirmation that pale malt was the more cost-effective commodity, porter brewers began using a blend of the cheaper pale malt and the new colored malts. Porter was the first beer not to be defined by the characteristics of the raw ingredients. The first beer to be mass produced, porter was *designed* by the brewer to fit a certain profile and fill a certain consumer niche, rather than being driven by the available raw materials and processes.

This simple base- and specialty-malt method of formulation was quickly adopted by all segments of the brewing industry, and today it is still the standard practice. Ironically, the very technology and innovation that spawned the porter style eventually destroyed it and cleared the way for mild ale to replace it.

What's in a Name?

It is important to remember that in the middle of the nineteenth century, the original ale—the unhopped malt liquor of the Angles, Saxons, Jutes, Normans, and the indigenous people of the British Isles—had been completely extinct for almost two centuries. Likewise the term *beer* no longer identified the hopped malt liquor as opposed to an unhopped ale. In the 1800s, *all* malt liquors were hopped, and the original designations were lost and became almost synonymous.

The meanings of *ale* and *beer* further mutated in the later eighteenth century, when porter and stout became popular, especially in the cities. With the rise of these new beverages, *ale* (which had almost entirely fallen from popular use) was resurrected and used to identify the common malt beverages still widely produced and consumed in the country. Although brown in color, these country ales were not nearly as dark as the mass-produced porters and stouts. However, they were neither as bitter nor as light in color as the "pale ales" that were gaining favor in some parts of the country. The term *beer* was commonly used to refer to porter and stout, while the term *ale* referred to the brown, mild products of the country and the newer pale beers.

The ambiguity of these definitions was further compounded by the way pubs used them to identify contemporary brews. Somewhere along the way between the decline of porter brewing and the rise of pale ale and subsequently bitter, the terms *mild* and *ale* seemed to have been used interchangeably, with the term *ale* pre-

Although it's called a dark ale, Northerner No. 1 was a very popular mild in West Yorkshire.

dominating. *Mild* was used when there was a possibility for confusion between a "mild ale" and a "pale ale." This is evidenced by the use of the terms *ale, porter,* and *stout* together on pub signs. In a slightly later period, the terms *pale, mild, porter,* and *stout* were often used together, but *ale* and *mild* were never listed as two separate products on the same sign.

These differences and similarities in beer styles silently mutated throughout the centuries. Today, the term *beer* is an umbrella term used to describe all nondistilled malt liquors. *Ale* is a class of beer that is hopped and fermented at relatively warm temperatures, typically with a top-fermenting yeast—the main feature that differentiates it from lagers, the newcomers on the scene. Mild ale is typically, though not always, the lowest-gravity beer in a brewery's portfolio. Both porters and stouts are generally classed within the ale category because they are usually made with a top-fermenting yeast, although some porters and stouts are made with a bottom-fermenting yeast.[21]

Beer, ale, porter, stout, pale, mild, bitter. The stylistic and categorical lines are hazy at best. Each term can imply a different commodity, yet they are often used in common conversation as generic terms referring to the same types of products under the broader genus of malt liquor.

The Road to the Modern Mild

There can be no greater challenge in the study of history than understanding changes in public tastes over the centuries, and the brewing industry has certainly proved that axiom to be true. The sources clearly show that there were fluctuations in consumer preferences significant enough to inspire both major and, presumably, minor brewers to change their product lines. Changes in social habits, the economic climate, temperance reforms, and taxation policies all impacted these shifts. But the degree of change in the characteristics of the primary beers—porter, stout porter, strong, stale (or old), mild, and pale ale—and the specific factors that motivated these changes are next to impossible to pin down and any explanation offered would be necessarily incomplete.

Porter, the beer market behemoth of the eighteenth and early nineteenth centuries, was to be confronted by a critical stumbling block in the very technology that helped create it. The rise in the popularity of gin was part of porter's fall from favor, but the black malt that the porter brewers were using as a coloring agent may have introduced a harsh, charcoal-like dry taste to the beer that had not been there before. The altered taste was surely instrumental in hastening the general shift in consumer preferences toward other beverages—including the new rival, pale ale.

So loathed was gin consumption by the legislators in Britain that they tried to enact laws to encourage the drinking of beer instead. The Beerhouse Act of 1830 entitled just about anyone to sell beer from a public house or even from their home under a license that cost just under £2. Suddenly pubs were everywhere. This helped boost beer sales over those of the rival gin, but it hurt porter as a style. The large porter breweries like Whitbread and Barclay and Perkins owned large numbers of pubs where their products were sold exclusively and the proliferation of free-trade outlets diluted their in-house market.[22]

Despite the decline in popularity that porter experienced, it still had a firm hold on the market. In 1833, Charrington's, one of the great mild producers of the time, began brewing porter, and as late as 1863, porter still made up 75% of all beer drunk in London.[23] This is not to say that the big brewers did not see the writing on the wall: The largest brewers, who owed their size and profitability to porter and the technology that came with it, began to produce mild ale. A witness to the 1833 Committee on the Sale of Beer observed that the typical London beer drinker was having "nothing but what is mild, and that has caused a considerable revolution in the trade, so much so that Barclay and Perkins and other great houses, finding that there is a decrease in the consumption of porter, and an increase in the consumption of ale, have gone into the ale trade; nearly all the new trade is composed of mild ale."[24]

From such accounts we can speculate that these ales were simply unaged beers of every hue. If it is true that Londoners of the time were demanding mild ales with such ferocity, even though porter still held a great portion of the marketplace, perhaps porter underwent a significant shift in flavor profile during those years. It may be that the porters of the mid–nineteenth century were more akin to the mild ales of that period than to the porters of a century before.

Until the 1870s at least, porter and mild battled for supremacy in the London area. A visitor to Cobb's Margate Brewery in 1875 remarked, "It is strange how the taste . . . for old stale beer has turned to the opposite extreme in the liking for mild and sweet by the present generation."[25] But by 1890, the trend turned away from vatted porter (which itself was becoming more and more "mild," in that it was vatted for a much shorter time—sometimes for as little as two months) toward the sweeter and less tart mild ale. One chronicler of the brewing industry noted that "the fickle public has got tired of the vinous flavoured vatted porter and transferred its affections to the new and luscious mild ale."[26]

The next great shift in public taste was the rise in popularity of pale ale—the beer that would at first compete with and finally replace mild ale as the beer of choice in Britain. As the use of glass drinking vessels became more widespread, the consumer began to place a high value on the brightness of the beer instead of its strength. The railroads that spanned Britain in the 1840s made the bright Burton ales far more accessible to people living in the cities, especially London. This new ale was very pale in color as compared to most mild ales and certainly to porter. Selling at prices one-third higher than porter or mild, the new pale ale was not a cheap drink; it found favor with the growing middle class. Although these beers—both mild and pale—were as heavily hopped as the vatted porter they replaced, they were not as strong and were not aged for long periods like porter. This trend in British beer was unique, as the rest of Europe and even the United States and the colonies switched from strong ales to weaker, bright golden lagers.

By the 1870s porter and strong beer had almost entirely lost favor in the cities, except among the older folk who had been weaned on the drink. Rural areas like Southwest England, the Midlands, and Suffolk also remained loyal to the old, strong ales. As the turn of the century approached, customers were increasingly demanding bottled beers, and brewers began to filter and carbonate their products for packaging. The brewers tried to capture as much of the market as possible by offering as many as ten or twelve different products in varying colors and strengths—stout, pale, bitter, porter, and mild ales. The weaker end of this range was still very high in gravity by present standards. In the *Art of Brewing*, published in 1875, the typical gravity of a mild is listed as 1.070, higher than the average gravity of a porter![27]

A 1905 treatise of the brewing industry described the beers that were available in Edwardian Britain:

. . . they may be divided into strong, medium and light. In the strong, we may include stock or old ales, and heavier stouts. The medium, comprises the lighter stouts, superior bitter beers, mild or four [pence] ale, which the latter is still the beverage of the working classes, and porter. The light beers . . . A good example of this type of beer is the so-called "family ale," and cheap kinds of bottled bitter beers and porters.[28]

From 1880 on, the trend toward paler, weaker, less-heavily hopped beers from the sweeter and heavier milds is driven by increased taxation, which by then was based upon the original gravity of the wort. Frequent wars necessitated the rationing of raw materials and drove taxes even higher. Writing in 1909, one observer noted that the average gravity for mild ale worts was 1.057 SG in 1880. By 1889 it had dropped to 1.055 SG, and by 1907 it had dropped even farther to around 1.048 SG. This drop of 15 to 20% over a 27-year period led the writer to conclude that "British working-man's beer of to-day is already practically a temperance beverage."[29] In 1902, Truman's brewery compared the gravities of its mild to those of its competitors. The gravities ranged from 1.038 SG to 1.059 SG, with an average of 1.048 SG.

Also, beginning in the 1870s brewers were quickly catching on to technological advances, and suddenly they were able to brew a wider range of fast-maturing beers nearly year-round. "Improved systems of brewing cause beers to mature in a period that would have astonished our grandfathers," wrote a

visitor to Northampton Brewing Company in 1875, "and old ales are now drunk that have been brewed in less time than was of old required to make the sweetest and mildest ales even moderately drinkable, and men of the time of the Whitbreads, the Meaux's and Calverts . . . would turn in their graves could they learn that their successors have their beers fit for consumption in less time than it took to fill their gigantic tuns."[30]

Modern Mild: The Last Hundred Years

Mild ale was to take another significant turn in the late nineteenth and early twentieth centuries. As the practice of aging ales for long periods of time fell from popularity, the term *mild ale* began to refer to beers that were malty and brown in color.[31] *The American Handy-Book of Brewing,*

Malting and Auxiliary Trades, which was published in 1908, describes milds as having a "more sweetish (mild) taste, containing more unfermented malto-dextrines and less acid [than stock beers]." The text goes on to list "London four ale (mild)" at 13–14 °Balling (1.053–1.057 SG).[32]

Whether these beers gradually became lighter in body and alcohol because brewers sought to reduce their costs or because consumers genuinely preferred them over higher-gravity beers is subject to debate. However, by the 1920s, the brown beers known as mild ales were so different from what they had been, only decades before, that

Photo courtesy of Brian Glover

Welsh miners–their faces black with coal dust–enjoy a few pints after a long day in the pits near Cwmback. In Wales, mild ale is simply called "dark."

Newcastle revived the term *brown ale* (which had fallen from popular use) to distinguish their higher-gravity product from the lower-gravity products being marketed under the name mild ale. The great success of this bottle-only product prompted a mad rush by other brewers to capitalize upon it. In this period between the World Wars, a great many British brewers introduced bottled beers under the name brown ale, though very few actually brewed a separate product for marketing under that name. Rather, they simply bottled their mild ales under the new moniker. The effects of this somewhat deceptive practice are still being felt today. Many breweries still bottle their mild ale under the name brown ale.

Even during the last half of the twentieth century mild lost ground both in gravity and in market share. In 1940, the popular English treatise *Brewing Science and Practice* listed grist bills for two mild ales: one at 1.040 SG, and one at 1.045 SG.[33] The Second World War delivered another blow to the average gravity and market share of mild ale. In 1940, mild accounted for almost 50% of the beer produced and consumed in England, but the consumption of bitter had been on the rise for decades, and it appeared that it might soon replace mild, just as porter had been replaced by mild a century earlier. When the British economy was forced to gear up for war in mainland Europe in 1941, the government once again restricted the flow of raw materials to the brewers, severely rationing barley. Large companies that operated several different breweries received the same allocation of barley for each of their plants as singular companies with only one plant. The larger companies that operated many breweries with different brand names, like Bass Charrington's and Whitbread, were able to redistribute raw materials among their individual breweries, thereby saving some brands and sacrificing others by lowering their gravities. Bass Pale Ale, for instance, remained at the same gravity as it had been prior to the war, but a smaller Bass-owned brewery, Tadcaster Tower Brewery, was forced to reduce the strength of their mild and bitter to make up for it. The brands that suffered were, of course, those whose market shares were already declining—such as porter and mild, which were losing out to bitter and pale.

This reduction in strength prompted the few consumers still drinking mild to switch to bitter simply because mild was no longer the drink they were used to. In isolated pockets, however, like the West Midlands, Greater Manchester, Southern Wales, and Northern England, mild remained popular with the manual laborers, who could quaff great quantities of the low-gravity beer after a hard day in the mine or factory and still be able to make conversation with their wives after the pub closed. By 1960, the average gravity of mild ale was 1.038 SG, and it would eventually fall farther yet.[34]

Ironically, the staunch loyalty of the working class to mild ale dealt what might be considered mild ale's final blow. Rebelling against their parents and grandparents' cloth-cap mentality, the newest generation is reaching for the new imported or domestic lagers. Lagers are bright, straw-colored, and fizzy; they are the alcoholic antithesis to the older generation's way of life. In 1980, mild accounted for 11% of draught beer sales in Britain, behind bitter at 44% and lager at 24%.[35] Today the sales of mild ale account for less than 4% of the beer bought and consumed in Britain.

Mild Today—And into the New Millennium

It is interesting to note that, although today's mild ale accounts for only a small fraction of the world's beer production, in the historical sense, mild accounts for nearly every beer in the world. Almost categorically, modern beer is served young, without the lactic sourness and *Brettanomyces* character that was the hallmark of the aged beers of centuries past.

Courtesy of Dennis Rutledge

With the exception of a few Belgian styles that are aged for long periods in wooden containers, the only remaining true "stale" ale is produced by Greene King of Bury St. Edmund's in Suffolk. This beer, called Old 5X, is aged in untreated, unlined 120-barrel oak vats covered in the local soil, called Suffolk Marl, which acts as a natural anti-microbial, anti-fugal agent during a year or more of aging. The beer is then blended with a younger product called BPA and marketed as Suffolk Strong. It is the closest thing contemporary drinkers have to an authentic eighteenth-century strong ale. Gale's Prize Old Ale is another excellent example of an aged stale beer, but the aging usually lasts only six months at the longest, and it does not take place in unlined wood containers. The flavors are nevertheless authentic, with a very delicate maltiness punctuated by a horsey sourness from lactic bacteria and wild yeasts.

As we have seen, the mild ale style has evolved dramatically over the centuries. At first, it referred to the entire class of beers that had not undergone a long aging process.

Then it was used to differentiate a beer from a pale or old ale, when contemporary beer culture no longer required the original designation. Finally, it lost gravity due to political, social, and economic forces and became the low-gravity, but flavorful, malty session beer we know today.

Mild continues to lose ground at an alarming rate. It is now confined to small pockets in England and to craft-brewing circles in the United States. It seems that one British brewer or another makes the decision to discontinue its mild ale every couple of months. Especially in this era of revivalist brewing, it would be a shame if mild ale—arguably the style from which all other English beers sprang—should disappear. It has made the trek down a long road pitted against lagers, marketing departments, and world wars only to reach this crossroad. Will mild take the road less-traveled and begin an upswing to newfound popularity or will it slowly fade into history?

Label Design by Eric Klosky

Fortunately, the future looks bright for mild ale. There are still a good many interesting examples of mild ale available, ranging from the viscous and caramelized Dark Ruby Mild from Sedgley's Sarah Hughes Brewery to the chocolatey, full-bodied Dark Mild from Walsall and High-gate in Dudley or the pale, malty Original AK from McMullen's in Hertfordshire. And the number of new milds appears to be growing. There were more mild entries at the Great American Beer Festival and the Craft Beer Institute's Real Ale Festival in Chicago in 1998 than in previous years. In addition, the *1998 CAMRA Good Beer Guide* lists more milds being produced in the United Kingdom than in previous editions, and the legions of dedicated craft- and homebrewers are making more milds than ever.

The beauty of mild as it exists today is in its simplicity. The lighter side of dark beers, it is light in body and alcohol, yet full of flavor and complexity. It is a simple beer to make, but an extremely difficult style to pin down. And while it is not likely that mild will become the top-selling beer in every brewery's portfolio any time soon, it will survive, thanks to the dedication of a few brewers who are as passionate about the style as they are about their craft.

CHAPTER 2

The Flavor Profile of Mild Ale

Mild ale as it exists at the latter half of the twentieth century is a difficult style to define. It has existed in one form or another for the whole of British brewing history. It has evolved into three distinct subcategories, each of which covers a great deal of territory: dark mild, which accounts for the vast majority of mild ales produced both in the United Kingdom and elsewhere; pale mild; and throwback mild, which includes milds that are more characteristic of the milds of years past. Indeed, it is difficult to describe a beer that can be at once light or dark, very low or very high in alcohol, and either rich in dark malt flavor and mouthfeel or light and crisp with a touch of hop flavor and aroma.

The first and second categories of mild ale are both modern. The first, the dark milds, are by far the most common commercially available milds. These ales use one or more dark specialty malts in their grist bill in addition to crystal malt, a pale base malt and, very often, a nongrain adjunct like brewers' caramel or invert sugar. The second category, the pale mild, is best exemplified by McMullen's Original AK. Pale milds are characterized by their maltiness and lack of dark malt in the grist bill. Typically, a pale mild will be in the same color range as a bitter or pale ale, but it will have less gravity and certainly less bitterness.

The original gravities of dark and pale mild ales are always below 1.040 SG; they average out at 1.034 SG. The color of dark milds generally falls between 11 and 100 degrees Standard Reference Method (°SRM), with an average of 43 °SRM.[1] Pale milds fall under 11 °SRM, with an average of 6. Bitterness levels in both pale and dark milds fall between 15 and 33 international bitterness units (IBUs), with an average of 23.[2]

The final category and, I believe, the truest category in terms of the historical roots of the style is that of the throwback mild. These milds exhibit one or more of the characteristics of milds as they existed decades or centuries ago. The most famous throwback mild is certainly Dark Ruby Mild from Sarah Hughes Brewery in Sedgley, West Midlands. With an original gravity (OG) of 1.058 or higher, a deep russet color, and a thick, sweet character, this mild is surely a clear depiction of what milds were like at the turn of the twentieth century. Throwback milds can be representative of any period in British brewing history, but they should be based both upon the raw materials available to the brewers of the time and upon the technology that was being used then.

As with most modern English beers, a significant proportion of the fermentable sugars in most milds comes from straight sugar added to the copper or from adjunctive grains. This means that these milds will have even lower body and flavor profiles than their original gravity might suggest. These are low-alcohol, low-bodied, yet full-flavored beers (see table 1).

Color and Clarity

Unlike other beer styles, mild ale can assume any color in the spectrum. The palest examples like McMullen's Original AK measure as little as 3 degrees Lovibond (°L)

TABLE 1

Mild Ale Profiles

Specifications	Throwback Mild	Dark Mild	Pale Mild
Original gravity	1.040–1.100	1.030–1.040	1.030–1.040
Apparent final gravity	1.012–1.030	1.006–1.008	1.005–1.008
Apparent degree of attenuation	60–80%	75–85%	75–85%
Real degree of attenuation	50–70%	58–70%	58–70%
Color (°SRM)	12–120	11–100	4–11
Bitterness	20–60	15–33	15–33
Alcohol % ABV	5.5–12%	3.5–4.3%	3.5–4.3%

and the darkest—Highgate Mild, for example—are upwards of 100 °L.

As is often the case in the modern British brewing world, the color is imparted by artificial coloring agents, rather than solely by dark malts and roasted barley. Holden's Mild and Banks's Mild are both darkened with the addition of caramel coloring at the end, as is the mild offering from Batham's—which the brewery admits is simply a colored version of their bitter. This is particularly sad because the brewery tap is the famous Bull and Bladder pub, on the facade of which is painted the most famous tribute to mild ale. Sarah Hughes's

Dark Ruby Mild and the Highgate Mild are both rather dark and made without the use of coloring agents. These two beers are fuller-bodied and more flavorful than Batham's mild with far more dark malt character, as one would expect.

As for clarity, modern mild ales are most often found on draught, served cask-conditioned. This means that the beer has undergone a secondary (or tertiary) fermentation in the cask from which it is served and has been fined or clarified by means of an added fining agent like isinglass or gelatin. I will discuss cask conditioning and fining in greater detail in chapter 5.

In rare instances, mostly in the United States and Canada, mild ales are served after having been filtered and force-carbonated, but in either case, modern mild ale, like most British beers, is meant to be served bright, without any turbidity from yeast or protein haze.

Defining Mild Ale

English-Style Pale Mild Ale

English pale mild ales range from light amber to light brown in color. Malty sweetness dominates the flavor profile; there is little hop bitterness or flavor. Hop aroma can be light. Very low diacetyl flavors may be appropriate in this low-alcohol beer. Fruity-ester level is very low. Chill haze is allowable at cold temperatures.

English-Style Dark Mild Ale

"English dark mild ales range from deep copper to dark brown (often with a red tint) in color. Malty sweetness and caramel are part of the flavor and aroma profile while licorice and roast malt tones may sometimes contribute to the flavor and aroma profile. These beers have very little hop flavor or aroma. Very low diacetyl flavors may be appropriate in this low-alcohol beer. Fruity-ester level is very low."

—1998 Great American Beer Festival *Guidelines to Beer Style Guidelines and Medal Categories*

"Mild is a brown ale of low alcoholic strength . . . that is not particularly robust or hoppy; rather it is thirst-quenching, low in alcohol, flavorful and light-to medium-bodied. A small amount of black patent or chocolate malt adds color more than flavor.

> Original gravities: 1.032–1.036 (8–9 °P). Alcohol: 2.5–3.5 percent. Bitterness: 14–30 IBU. Color: 22–35 °SRM."
>
> —Charlie Papazian, *The New Complete Joy of Homebrewing*
>
> "[In *Brewing and Malting Science*] Hough et al. gives 'draught mild' at 1.031–1.037 (7.5–9.1 °P); alcohol 2.5–3.6 ABV, with 14–37 IBU bitterness."
> —Fred Eckhardt, *The Essentials of Beer Style*

Flavor, Body, and Aroma

Dark Mild

Dark mild is always tawny to black in color, perhaps with a garnet tint, and, therefore, most often has some caramel, chocolate, and coffee flavors, along with the associated roasted aromas. Because dark milds are frequently brewed with some adjunctive source of sugar, this tends to thin the body and diminish the malt flavors, though not to the point of making the beer insipid. Hop bitterness is most often very low so as to take the edge off the malty sweetness without affecting the overall malty character of the beer. Hop flavor and aroma is very light to imperceptible, with a few notable examples having a

AK: The Roots of Pale Mild

In the eighteenth, nineteenth, and early twentieth centuries, up to 100 breweries produced pale milds under the moniker AK. Today there are only two left. The most famous is McMullen's Original AK. Although many of the breweries that at one time produced an AK are still in business (Young's, Fuller's, McMullen's, and Ind Coope among them), they seem to have all forgotten what the name meant.

Theories, folklore, and humorous local appellations abound, however. Before and during the First World War, it was popularly believed that AK stood for "Asquith's knockout," after the British Prime Minister Herbert Asquith, who imposed the heaviest-ever tax on beer in Britain as a means of financing the war. Others believed that it stood for "after killing," as it was common for slaughterhouse workers to quaff a good many pints after a long day at work. Perhaps it is a bastardization of "ale conners" (konners), who were the first official beer inspectors.

What is more likely is that the moniker was first used by the brewers to distinguish the ale as suitable for a specific trade. It might have been an abbreviation for "amber-kitchen," to distinguish it as lesser-quality ale intended for the servants. Or, it might have stood for *ale kyte*, Flemish for "small beer."

Perhaps the best explanation harkens back to the days when all breweries used Xs to indicate levels of strength. The ales with the lowest alcohol would have had the fewest Xs. The beer with the lowest mark, but of premium quality, might have been marked with an "A" for quality, but only half an X —which would have looked an awful lot like a "K."

A nineteenth-century advertisement for Waltham Brothers Brewery (see page 60) seems to support this theory. It lists prices for X, XX, XXX, and even an XXXX Strong Mild Ale, along with a product designated "AK" that was among the lowest in price.

very pleasant floral, fresh-tobacco aroma imparted by Fuggle or Styrian Golding hops.

Pale Mild

Pale mild, as the name suggests, is very light in color as compared to the dark milds and is often very similar to the color of bitters and pale ales. The difference here lies both in the character of the beer in terms of maltiness versus hoppiness and, most substantially, in terms of the beer's gravity. Pale and bitter ales are typically in the range of 1.040 to 1.055 SG, whereas beers termed or considered pale milds are always of lower gravity than that.

Where this line becomes hazy, as in the case of Federation Special Ale from Tyne and Wear, England, which weighs in at 1.033 SG (clearly inside the mild ale gravity parameters), hoppiness becomes the defining characteristic. Federation has a wonderful bouquet imparted by Brambling Cross hops that is reminiscent of Boddington's Pub Ale from Manchester, England—another, more popularly known ale that has often been listed as a pale mild.

Pale milds, of course, lack the chocolate and toffee flavors of their dark mild counterparts; they also have a crisper, sometimes biscuit-like pale malt signature. The aroma—lacking the overpowering roasted notes associated with dark malts—is fruitier and more subtle than the darks. Hop aroma is not unheard of, but it is always secondary to the malt.

It should be noted here that many brewers of pale mild have succumbed to marketing forces and have begun to call their products by the more market-friendly moniker *bitter*. McMullen's of Hertfordshire, England, which makes Original AK—known for well over a century as a pale mild—has recently begun calling their ale a light bitter. And Boddington's is calling its pale mild, at 1.035 original gravity (OG), simply a pub ale.

Throwback Mild

There are a few examples of mild ale that have not changed with the times—they have become living examples of mild ale's potent past. By far the most famous is Sarah Hughes' Ruby Mild, which is brewed with a recipe that dates back to the first quarter of the twentieth century. This beer is very fruity, with a bold body and mouthfeel. Cooked fruit, vanilla, and caramel round out the palate, with a slight buttery note from trace diacetyl. The aroma is at once floral and spicy, from Fuggle and Whitbread Goldings hops, and the beer finishes with a pleasant bitterness and a touch of acidity. Though it is likely that Dark Ruby Mild would have been at home among the milds of a century ago, it is most akin to some of the modern old ales produced by Northeastern English breweries like Greene King and Nethergate.

SARAH HUGHES BREWERY

ORIGINAL HOME BREWED ALES

DARK RUBY

O.G. 1058
ABV 5.8%

Another throwback mild is Merrie Monk from Marston, Thompson, and Evershed in Burton-on-Trent. The deputy head brewer, John Cheetham, calls Merrie Monk (one of the offerings in the Head Brewer's Choice line of beers) a dark mild, it is fuller in body and higher in gravity than other Midlands milds. Merrie Monk is chocolatey and sweet, with only the faintest hint of hops and a rare oakiness—no doubt a quality attributable to the Burton Union sets still in use at the brewery. It is in those unions that Merrie Monk and Marston's other mild, Walnut Mild, are wholly fermented.

Several other British breweries make products they call milds that do not fall in the realm of low-gravity beers. Perhaps the most extreme example of a throwback mild is brewed by the Bull Mastiff Brewery in Cardiff, Wales. Their Ebony Dark Mild, weighing in at 1.073 SG—18.25 degrees Plato (°P)—and 7.0% ABV is almost opaque black but reveals a garnet tinge when held to the light. One expects the first sip of this mighty brew to be awash with coffee and roasted flavors but, strangely, the flavor is incongruous with the color, revealing only pleasant toffee and licorice notes, with a nice hop balance from what is almost certainly a heavy dose of Golding.

Because mild ale is found in such a wide spectrum of colors and flavors, it is among the hardest styles to pin down to well-defined style guidelines. This difficulty is among the chief reasons for the decline of mild ale. As the flavor, aroma, and color profiles of other styles such as bitter, old ale, and brown ale have become more easily definable and those styles have become lower in gravity than their earlier versions, the style parameters for mild ale are being absorbed by these other styles. What was once clearly a pale mild might today be just as easily termed a bitter (for example, McMullen's Original AK, at 1.033 OG), and what could have twenty years ago been called a dark mild is today known as an old ale (for example, Adnam's Old Ale, at 1.037 OG).

CHAPTER 3

Mild Ale Ingredients

Malt, water, and hops are the three requisites for brewing ale.

—Alfred Barnard, *The Noted Breweries of Great Britain and Ireland, Vol. II*

Because mild ale is essentially English, it only makes sense to use raw ingredients that are English as well. And although it is true that some of the strains of barley grown and malted in Great Britain are also grown and malted in the United States and elsewhere and that some varieties of hops cultivated in the United States and elsewhere are descendants of original English stock, the simple fact is that it is *not* the same. This is not to say that British raw materials are the quintessential ingredients for beer or that American raw materials are intrinsically inferior; rather this recognizes that because mild ale has such delicacy of flavors that the brewer must take great care in ensuring that the ingredients used are employed by design and not as a matter of habit or convenience.

Malt

> The best malt will make the best ale, and it is cheapest in the end; as by using it, there is but little danger in the process of brewing good beer.
>
> —Alfred Barnard, *The Noted Breweries of Great Britain and Ireland, Vol. II*

Mild ales of all types should feature malt as the signature flavor. Even those examples that have a noticeable hop presence should not forgo malt in favor of hops. At the risk of sounding overly poetic, the malt should be the tree from whose branches all other flavors hang from like ornaments. Because of the typically low gravity and delicate profile of mild ale, the types of malt you use—with no exception made for the base malt—will profoundly impact the final character of the beer.

Mild ales typically consist of a pale malt base, some crystal or caramel malt, and, in the case of dark milds, a colored malt such as chocolate, black, or roasted. In addition to these products, we will consider mild ale malt and brown malt, as well as some adjunctive grains like corn and oats.

Pale Malt

As with all other British styles of beer, pale malt is the soul of the grist bill. It is, by far, the main source of fermentable sugar and a significant factor in the flavor profile. Pale malts of British origin are highly modified; conversion takes place quickly and yields as much fermentable sugar as possible given the amount of malt used and the temperature of conversion. Pale malt made by some American maltsters from six-row barley should be avoided, as the modification possible with this barley does not lend itself to single-temperature infusion mashing. It produces a definite difference in flavor and texture as compared to British two-row malts. Also, because we do not have the benefit of a protein rest, a malt with low protein levels is recommended.

British pale malts are readily available, and most maltsters produce their pale malts to very similar specifications in modern, highly controlled maltings. The exception to this rule is the traditional floor maltings that most agree produce some of the best malt in the world.

Rather than the typical American concern with the manufacturer of the malt, British brewers seem to be more particular about the variety (or cultivar) of barley that is used. Depending upon the maltster and the preferences of

its larger customers, your malt may be of the Pipkin, Halycon, Plumage Archer, or Golden Promise varieties. Marris Otter, a winter barley, is the type most commonly selected to malt by hand in a floor maltings. Floor-malted barley has found few critics; in fact, it is widely held to be the best malt available to both the British brewer and the American home- or craftbrewer. While there is a romantic quality to using malt that has truly been handcrafted, there is a better reason to use it—flavor, the simplest and most important malt analysis.

Pale malts are generally crisp and biscuit-like in flavor. Any sour notes or stale flavors indicate that the malt has gone bad, and it should not be used. Floor-malted Maris

Otter is even more biscuit-like, and although it tastes similar to regular pale malt from Crisp, Muntons, or Paul's, it possesses more depth of character. This difference does, without question, translate into the finished product, especially when the product is intended to be malty—like a mild ale.

Crystal or Caramel Malt

Caramel and crystal are used interchangeably to describe malt that is made by taking properly germinated green malt, soaking it to near 50% moisture, subjecting it to conditions that cause the endosperm to sacchrify and liquefy (basically the equivalent of mashing the grain), and heating the entire kernel so that the sugary liquid caramelizes and becomes unfermentable. As it cools, the liquid center of the barley corn hardens into a crystalline structure (hence the British name for the malt) that can be dissolved into the wort via the mash later in the brew house. (See the section "Kilning and Roasting Your Own Grains" later in this chapter.)

Depending upon the quantity of this malt in the formula, the brewer can achieve colors from a slightly orange-gold through copper and into the realm of brown. In addition to being a coloring agent, crystal malt also imparts quite a bit of flavor and body to the character of the beer. Crystal malts are available from 20 to 120 °L. The lightest malt in the crystal category is dextrin or Cara-Pils. Dextrin is about 1 to 10 °L in color and is used in relatively small quantities when little color or flavor is desired but the increased body and heavier mouthfeel that crystal malt imparts are.

Used in the proper amounts, crystal malt will impart a malty sweetness that is difficult to achieve otherwise. Also, because the sugars extracted from crystal malt are largely unfermentable, they will be present in the product after fermentation is complete, improving the beer's overall body, mouthfeel, and head retention.

Crystal malt is perfect for extract brewing. Because the malt is essentially pre-mashed in the malting process, the sugars are already available for dissolution in water. Steeping the malt in hot water (165 °F, 73.5 °C) before adding the extract will produce nearly the same effect as adding it to a full mash profile.

Chocolate and Black Malt

Chocolate and black malt are prepared in much the same way, except that some of the starches in malt destined to become chocolate malt are allowed to sacchrify before the grain is roasted to a very dark color (400–500 °L) in a drum roaster. Temperature, moisture, and the mixing action of the cylindrical drum roaster are essential to the successful production of these malts because the intense heat and prolonged roasting time can induce a runaway reaction that turns the barley into charcoal. Black malt (500+ °L) yields an acrid, burnt, but not unpleasant flavor, while chocolate malt imparts more sweetish, roasted notes. Each of these malts should be employed in small amounts in a dark mild, more for color than for the flavor they will invariably impart.

Roasted Barley and Roasted Malt

Like chocolate and black malt, roasted barley is prepared in a cylindrical drum roaster. Although the color of roasted barley is similar to that of black malt (450–600 °L), the barley is both unmalted and roasted with a greater moisture content, producing a drier, sharper flavor than found in other dark malts.

Roasted malt is chiefly made by continental maltsters who wish to offer a product with the characteristics of roasted barley that still conforms to the *Reinheitsgebot*—the German beer purity law of 1516. That law mandated that brewers may only use four ingredients in making beer: malted barley, water, hops, and yeast. Though the law was later expanded to include malted wheat, it has continued to exclude unmalted cereal grains. The malt used in the production of continental roasted malt is called chit malt. Steeped for a very short time and kilned very lightly, it is quite undermodified.

Guinness has used roasted barley and roasted malt interchangeably in their recipes for some markets. So far, the brewers have not been able to detect a taste difference between the two.[1]

Mild Ale Malt

Mild ale malt is something of an enigma. The maltsters who make a product under this name say that it is used specifically for the production of mild and brown ales, but I have been unable to find a single mild ale brewer who will admit to using it. One of the brewers I spoke to was so puzzled when I mentioned mild ale malt, that he spent 20 minutes trying to explain that pale malt was not just for pale ales—that it was used in their mild ales as well. In retrospect, I probably shouldn't have gone on to ask whether he had ever used Baird's stout malt.

I can find one reference to mild ale malt in Michael Jackson's *Beer Companion* where he lists it as an ingredient in a milk stout.[2] Beyond that, I have found very few references in modern brewing or malting texts, and even these offer scant information. One British maltster claims that the product was developed for the British market, but didn't sell, and it was revived for the American small-scale brewing trade, where everyone is always waiting for the next big thing from Europe.

Mild ale malt does, nevertheless, fill an interesting niche in the world of base malts. The typical analysis suggests that it is a little more dextrinous than the average pale malt and perhaps a bit darker. Unlike CaraPils or dextrin malt, mild ale malt retains plenty of diastatic power for sacchrification. It is usually malted from the Triumph variety of barley—a barley of slightly lower quality for malting.

Brown Malt

If mild ale malt is an enigma, brown malt is a complete mystery. Brown malt, sometimes also called "blown malt," is the malt most closely associated with the porters of the past. It was most assuredly used in the mild ales of earlier times. The best description of the malting process for brown malt can be found in a mid-nineteenth-century English brewing text.[3] The passage describes laying the malt out at a depth of about one-half inch on the floor of

Roasting Your Own Grains

One of the biggest problems with brewing recipes converted from old recipe books is that the main ingredients (malt and hops) are unavailable today. Although the best we can do for antique hops, short of cultivating and selecting our own varieties, is to use the modern standards that have replaced them, we *can* closely approximate the malts brewers of past centuries would have used in their beers.

Home-roasted grains add a depth of flavor, aroma, and color that would be otherwise unachievable in a beer brewed only with stock malts. Roasting grains involves spreading a layer about 1 inch deep on a baking pan that easily accommodates at least 1 pound of grain. The simplest roast of pale malt in a 350 °F (176.5 °C) pre-heated oven for 10 minutes will bring out a light caramel, malty flavor. Roast the malt for longer (20 to 30 minutes) to produce an amber-colored malt with some, albeit very little, diastatic power. Remember to monitor the roast for aroma and flavor, and stir the grains frequently to avoid burning.

A long roast will turn the malt brown. This is somewhat similar to modern brown malts in that it produces a brown color with no diastatic activity. However, the flavor and aroma is far more complex than the commercially available variety.

> My solution to the historical brown malt dilemma is to use a mixture of home-roasted malts: 40% lightly roasted, 30% medium-roasted amber malt, and 30% heavy-roasted brown malt. The brown malt of past centuries was cured over a hardwood fire and invariably picked up some of the smoke reek as a result. To add another dimension to your approximation of historical brown malt, smoke the entire 40-30-30 blend over some hardwood in a home smoker, or add a small percentage (5% or so) of German *Rauchmalz* or peat-smoked malt.

the malt kiln—which was constructed with a steel false bottom with a fire box below it. A hardwood fire was lit in the fire box, and the temperature of the grain would rapidly rise to 180 °F (82 °C). This passage also suggests that the malt picked up a great deal of flavor from the fire.

During this kind of curing, three things are almost certain to occur. First, reek from the fire would settle on the malt and impart to the beer made from it a characteristically smoky flavor and aroma (although no source actually uses the term *smoky* when describing the "peculiar flavor so much esteemed by the porter drinker").[4] Second, a significant proportion of the barley corns would pop, or torrify, like popcorn, no doubt giving rise to the moniker "blown malt." Third, and central to the mystery of brown malt, is that kilning as described above would almost certainly destroy any enzymatic potential the malt might have had. At best, the enzymes would have been severely reduced in quantity.

Because brown malt is listed in numerous sources as the bulk of the grist charge in early porters—if not the sole constituent—there must have been another mitigating factor. It is reasonable to guess that the brown malt may have first been wetted and the endosperm allowed to sacchrify and liquefy, as in the modern production of crystal malt. If the heat were not allowed to become too intense, it is possible that a significant amount of fermentable sugars would have survived and remained in the malt, in which case only minimal amounts of diastase would have been required.

Also, it is possible that the wort resulting from a brown malt mash would have been quite glutinous—full of dextrines and perhaps some starch. These compounds, unfermentable by normal beer yeasts, would have been easily attacked by invading lactic bacteria and *Brettanomyces* during the aging process. This would have reduced the unfermentable sugars into alcohol and produced the sour tartness that was the hallmark of ales before the end of the nineteenth century. A very good approximation of historical brown malt can be made at home in your oven (see the sidebar, "Roasting Your Own Grains").

A few words about modern, commercially produced brown malt: It has no diastatic power and imparts a nice brown hue not unlike that obtainable with chocolate malt, but with a different flavor profile. In small proportions (no more than 10% of the total grist charge), it produces light biscuit flavors with perhaps a hint of roastiness. This is an interesting malt to experiment with, but as explained previously, do not attempt to use it as a base malt.

A number of sources have suggested that using some modern peat-smoked malt or German *Rauchmalz* would result in a better interpretation of the brown malt of yore.

Adjuncts

Most modern milds, like most modern British beers in general, are produced using adjunctive sources of sugar including corn grits, oats, pure cane and invert sugar, and brewers' caramel. The historical reasons for using these adjuncts is largely economic in nature, but it would be short-sighted to say that they are categorically evil products that have no place in the brewing world. Adjuncts with low nitrogen contents, like corn and rice, can be used to correct malt with an unusually high nitrogen level;

adjuncts with high protein contents, like wheat, can aid head retention. As with different malts, hops, and the use of spices in some beers, adjuncts impart to the beer their own characters, which are not necessarily undesirable.

Adjuncts can be divided into three categories: those that are added to the mash, those that are added to the copper, and coloring adjuncts that are added to the finished beer. We will deal with all three in this section, limiting discussion to those adjuncts that are either typical in a mild ale brewery or that lend themselves well to the brewing of mild ale.

Mash Tun Adjuncts

The typical brewers' grist bill has not changed much in the last 50 years. Specialty beers and the philosophies of some breweries aside, the typical grist bill consists of approximately 75% malt, 10% mash tun adjuncts, and 15% copper adjuncts.[5] These figures are not meant to be a prescription for British beers in general nor for mild ale specifically; they are only meant to be representative of British brewing. Any brewer would be doing himself a disservice by mistaking the figures mentioned here for gospel truth and by failing to experiment with malts and adjuncts on his or her own. Adjuncts can give a whole new dimension to brewing mild ales—or any other style of beer, for that matter.

One note on the use of grain adjuncts: With the exception of wheat, whole, unprocessed grains cannot be used directly in the mash. These grains must be cracked (as through a mill) and cooked (mixed with water and boiled) to gelatinize their starches before they are added to the mash.

Flaked and rolled grains, on the other hand, are not cooked. The starches in these grains are gelatinized as a product of the heat and pressure of the roller mill. They are ready for the mash with no further preparation.

Corn and wheat. Corn is not indigenous to the British Isles. It does not grow well there, accounting for less than 12% of all acreage dedicated to raising crops. Therefore, it would not have been the first choice of adjunct among the British brewers of old. In modern times, a product called brewers' corn has found its way into many bitters and a few milds, but it is used only occasionally. It is commonly a mixture of smaller, British-grown kernels and imported kernels. Because a great deal of the corn must be imported, usually from the Americas, the mixture tends to be expensive. Nevertheless, it is a good adjunct that works well in a mild ale.

Corn, or maize, contributes fermentable sugars while lightening the character (color and body) of the beer. It adds a grainy sweetness and helps accentuate the character of the hops. Flaked maize is the best form to use because it is pregelatinized and ready for conversion. (It is a popular misconception that flaked corn can be used without the benefit of enzymatic action, such as the steeping of specialty grains. This is not true. However, for similar results, one can use corn sugar—that is, dextrose—added directly to the wort before boiling.)

Corn makes for a good, crisp beer, but I recommend reserving the use of this adjunct to beers of at least 1.036 SG (9 °P) and above. The lack of unfermentable sugars in the wort to create body and mouthfeel can cause the resulting beer to be thin and watery.

Wheat, like corn, lightens the body and color. Unlike corn, though, the typical protein levels are very high and may cause unwanted haziness. Wheat starch gelatinizes at relatively low temperatures (122–130 °F, 51.5–54 °C), so cooking unprocessed wheat is not necessary. Wheat is typically extraordinarily high in beta glucans (a sticky compound that is notorious for sticking mashes), so be careful. Although wheat (malted) is used for up to 80% of some grist bills for German *weizens*, and unmalted wheat is used for up to 50% of the grist bills (along with about 5% oats) in Belgian *wit* beers, I would not recommend anything above 10% for a mild ale.

Oats. Oats are most commonly found in oatmeal stouts and a few oatmeal pale ales, but I have seen a large quantity of oats used in other breweries, including one very large brewer of Irish stout and at least one mild ale brewery. The latter makes perfect sense. The oiliness or silkiness that oats impart to a beer is perfectly suited to mild ales, where perceived body and mouthfeel, along with wholesome flavors from grain, are of paramount importance.

Flaked oats are easiest to use and can be added directly to the mash, but the quantity should not exceed 15% of the grist weight. Oats, like wheat, contain high levels of beta glucans and can stick the mash rather handily. I am a great proponent of single-temperature infusion mashes, especially when brewing a mild ale, but if you find that using oats is too costly in terms of time and effort because they cause your mashes to stick, try a low-temperature rest (at 122–125 °F or 50–51.5 °C) to denature beta glucans before raising the mash temperature to achieve sacchrification.

Copper Adjuncts: Sugar and Invert Sugar

Copper adjuncts are water-soluble additives that typically represent up to 15% of the total original wort gravity. They usually take some form of sugar, and they are added to the wort sometime after the boil has started.

Sucrose is derived from the sugar cane, a giant tropical grass, and from the swollen root of the sugar beet. Refined, white sucrose and its hydrolysis product, invert sugar, are used in the vast majority of British breweries. Pure cane sugar and pure beet sugar have almost identical compositions and are indistinguishable from each other in their refined state and in a finished beer.

Impure, partially refined grades of beet sugar impart unpleasant flavors and aromas and are not used in brewing. Partially refined cane sugars, on the other hand, have pleasant flavors and aromas and might be desirable in a dark mild ale. These products include demerara or turbinado sugar, molasses (treacle), and golden syrup. These are common copper adjuncts in a variety of beer styles and have been used in the commercial brewing of mild ales in Britain and the United States. The fermentability of these adjuncts varies, though, and one might expect to yield about 90% for turbinado or demerara, 60% for molasses, and 80% for golden syrup.

Adding invert sugar to a batch of Dark Ruby Mild at Sarah Hughes. The sugar, which arrives at the brewery in 5-pound chunks, is put into a mesh basket and suspended in the open-top copper behind. The wood-insulated vessel in the foreground is the mash tun. Notice the wort shooting out of the bottom and into the copper.

Brown sugar was originally taken from the refinement process before the final bleaching, like modern turbinado sugar. In the United States today, however, brown sugar is simply refined cane sugar with a small percentage (less than 10%) molasses added back in.

Invert sugar is prepared by hydrolysis of disaccharide sucrose into its constituent monosaccharides, glucose and fructose, with a dilute acid solution or, rarely, by the use of the enzyme invertase. Invert sugar may be supplied to the brewer in the form of a syrup, or it might be even further reduced into a block. Each of these forms contain about 83% solids. Those solids are about 91 to 95% fermentable, depending upon the color; the darker, the less fermentable they are.

In order to be fermentable, sucrose must first be hydrolyzed by the yeast, which secretes invertase to do the job. Pure sucrose and invert sugar are equally metabolized by yeast, with no effect on beer flavor or aroma, but sucrose is often the preferred product because it is cheaper. Some brewers, however, still like invert sugar for priming because less yeast is needed in suspension to hydrolyze the sucrose. Often a mixture of 55% invert to 45% sucrose is used for this purpose.

All completely fermentable sugars, like sucrose or invert sugar, yield about 1.045 SG per pound of sugar to a U.S. gallon of water.

Coloring Adjuncts

It should be noted that many mild ale breweries in Britain use coloring agents to darken their mild ales after fermentation is complete and the beer is ready for packaging. Although this practice does not directly reflect poor character on the part of the brewer, I cannot recommend the use of coloring agents for this purpose. In fact, I wholeheartedly discourage it—it is tantamount to adding green food coloring to beer on St. Patrick's Day.

I suspect that this practice may be one of the many reasons that the consumption of mild ale has declined so dramatically in recent years. A good number of breweries, including one of the leading brewers of mild ale, is by all accounts guilty of brewing one beer and calling it bitter in its unadulterated form and mild if it is colored. The brewery claims that its customers don't know the difference and simply want a dark beer as opposed to a pale beer. Some have lamented this brewery's recent decision to drop the *mild* moniker as another chink in mild ale's haggard armor, but I think that mild ale as a style and those dedicated to saving it are better off without those who would cheapen and disrespect it.

Some breweries use caramel after fermentation to add some color and some sugar to the beer. I would not categorize this approach as belonging completely in the adjunct color column because the caramel does add to the beer's flavor profile as well. A tasting of beers before and after the addition of caramel confirms that the flavor is not the same—it actually benefits from the addition of caramel.

Hops

Foreign hops are out of the question, as the finest of that description will taint the Ale with an unpleasant twang, however carefully used. I tasted a sample of Ale brewed with the finest Bavarians, at the rate of twenty pounds per Barrel in the cask, to my surprise the bitter was scarcely perceptible, but it contained a most unpleasant bite on the throat, which lasted some time after being drank, it was deficient in that beautiful aroma to the nose; now with English hops you have a most agreeable smell, and no taste is left after being drank.

—George Stewart Amsinck
Practical Brewings: A Series of Fifty Brewings

There can be little doubt that hops of English descent have ideal characteristics for use in mild ale. Although hop presence is traditionally minimal in mild ale, this does not mean that the selection of hops is unimportant. The hops should round out the flavor of the beer, offset the cloying sweetness of the malt with bitterness without masking the maltiness, and provide a background character to ensure that the beer has sufficient depth. We will explore here the main varieties that are appropriate for use in mild ales.

The Golding Family:
East Kent, Kent, and B.C. Goldings

> A good Kent beats all.
>
> —George Stewart Amsinck
> *Practical Brewings: A Series of Fifty Brewings*

> Look strictly to the marks, East Kent, Mid Kent and Kent (Kent only, means Weald of Kent) . . . each of these marks carry more value than the other in the market. I have seen, not a few times, marked Mid Kent, from the following parishes, Tonbridge, Cranbrook, Hadlow, Brenchley, not one of these belong to Mid Kent, they are Wealds and ought to be marked Kent, naturally the purchaser is paying more than he ought to do, or if they are sold at Weald price, he imagines that he has got a bargain, at all events he is not buying what he supposes he is.
>
> —George Stewart Amsinck
> *Practical Brewings: A Series of Fifty Brewings*

Hops, as discussed previously, were first brought to the British Isles in the late fifteenth century. Until the eighteenth century, hop varieties were of strictly local significance. These crops, often bred from wild stock and the descendants of continental strains, were probably harsh and astringent.

By the mid-1700s, English farmers began selecting strains of hops for their aromatic, flavor, and bittering properties. Hundreds of varieties, still only locally grown and locally known, had been selected by 1750. In 1790, a farmer named John Golding chose a particular set of plants and based his entire hop-farming enterprise on that type of hops.

Today, the Golding family of hops consists of eight very similar varieties, including Brambling, Early Birds, and Mathons—each named for the farmer that selected them or the parish in which they were grown. Although similar in character, each of the varieties either matures at a different time or is more or less resistant to hop pests. When you purchase Goldings hops, whether they be East Kent, Kent, or some other type, you will be getting one of these varieties.

Regardless of the actual variety you get, if they were grown in the Eastern part of the County of Kent, they will be called East Kent Goldings (the variety that is widely considered to be the best). If they were grown elsewhere in Kent, they will be labeled simply Kent Goldings. If they were grown in British Columbia, Canada, they will be labeled BC Goldings. Grown anywhere else, they will simply be called Goldings.

Hops grown in each of these regions will produce a slightly different character even though they stem from the same stock. You must be aware of exactly what you are using in order to be sure that you can repeat the performance should you be happy with the results—or *not* repeat it, if you are unsatisfied.

Goldings are the pinnacle English aroma hop, with a gentle, floral aroma that is perfect for milds. Please note that Styrian or Savinjski Goldings are not a Golding variety but are instead descended from a Fuggle stock.

Fuggle

Pronounced fuh'-gull, this hop is second in popularity to the Golding varieties. First propagated from a seedling in 1875, it soon became the most popular hop in Britain. By 1950, it accounted for 78% of the British hop crop. Unfortunately, a widespread attack of *Verticillum* wilt later made production almost impossible, and today it represents only about 10% of the crop.

A large portion of the Fuggle crop is grown in the West Midlands, and therefore, it is used as the primary hop in a great many mild ales if for no other reason than that of proximity. English Fuggle are better than the American or Canadian varieties, contributing a tea-like or tobacco-like character that is very pleasant in a low-gravity, malty beer.

Brambling Cross

Bred from a Brambling (a Golding variety) and a wild male hop from Manitoba, Canada, Brambling Cross is an aroma hop with black currant and citrus notes. Brambling Cross has a deceptively low alpha-acid content and aroma in its fresh, whole-flower state. If used correctly, in small amounts for mild ale, Brambling Cross is a fantastic hop with very distinctive aroma and flavor characteristics.

Northern Brewer

Northern Brewer is a great mid-alpha hop for bittering. It does not add the harsh flavors that some other hops in this category can.

Willamette

Willamette is a seedless (triploid) American-grown hop cultivated from Fuggle stock that has a slightly different, but very good character of its own. It has a mild, sweet, and spicy character, not unlike and perhaps even preferable to that of English-grown Fuggle. I would recommend Willamette as one of the two non-English hops suitable for dry-hopping a mild ale. When used sparingly, Willamette imparts a very pleasant fresh-tobacco aroma and flavor.

Styrian Golding

Recent research shows rather conclusively that Styrian Goldings are also grown from Fuggle stock (in combination with the American Tettnanger) despite their misleading name.[6] Although analytically identical to Fuggle and American Tettnanger, Styrian or Savinjski Goldings have developed a distinctive mild and floral character of their own since their importation to Slovenia. This is a hop to be used often, but sparingly. I have had very good results using the whole flowers as a dry hop.

Brewing Liquor

For ales, well water, of the Burton type, bored down to the rock, like that at Springfield, is the most suitable for every decoction or maceration. The purer the water—that is—the freer from all organic substances, the better is the ale, and for this reason, modern brewers prefer using spring, to river water.

—Alfred Barnard, *The Noted Breweries of Great Britain and Ireland, Vol. II*

Possibly much the best Water in all England is that at Castleton in Derbyshire, commonly called The Devils Arss, &c. Which Owzes from a great Rock, covered over with a shallow Earth and short Grass a top.

—Richard Bradley
A Guide to Gentleman Farmers and Housekeepers for Brewing the Finest Malt Liquors

Being the largest constituent ingredient by both weight and volume, the quality of the brewing water will have a dramatic effect on the resulting beer. Although in direct disagreement with the information from the first passage above, the classic water for all brown, malty beers is London water. However, water treatment for mild ales differs significantly from brewery to brewery. Mild ale, being intrinsically entwined in the British brewing heritage has, over the course of centuries, been brewed in every corner of Britain and from every conceivable composition of water. Highgate and Walsall's water is very soft, so they do not treat it; they add salts for all their other beers. Marston's in Burton-on-Trent uses the same classically hard water for their milds as they do for their famous Pedigree Bitter.

Basically, if your water tastes good, you can brew with it. Brewing water should always be selected primarily for its purity and secondly for its mineral composition. You can reduce some of the hardness in your water by boiling it to precipitate calcium carbonate.

From a historical perspective, brewer and author Gregory Noonan quotes Robert Wallace of the Bass Crest Brewery in Alloa, Scotland, who recorded what he considered an ideal water analysis for mild ale in 1873. The analysis lists 288 mg/l calcium sulfate (gypsum), $CaCO_3$ (calcium carbonate) at 151 mg/l, NaCl (salt) at 4 mg/l, and a total hardness of 439 mg/l.[7]

This analysis is a bit harder than the classic London water at 235 mg/l hardness, but far softer than Burton water, which has 875 mg/l hardness.

Do not fret about your water—as I said earlier, if you can drink it, you can brew with it. If you want to toy with the composition of your water more than simply boiling it and adding a little gypsum for your pale ales, consult Gregory Noonan's *New Brewing Lager Beer* and *Scotch Ale,* as well as the other books listed in appendix C.

Yeast

> I saw in print somewhere, an opinion from some scientific gentleman, that pressed yeast would not do for the purpose of fermentation, because when the globules of the yeast are broken, the fermenting power was destroyed. I have used pressed yeast, and I know many who have done so, and the only difference I and they experienced, is, that it is necessary to take less in weight per Barrel, because there being no beer, there is more solid fermenting power, this does not prove the aforesaid theory, or perhaps the globules, whatever they are, in the instances I quote above, have not met the same fate.
>
> —George Stewart Amsinck
> *Practical Brewings: A Series of Fifty Brewings*

Whenever two or more brewers meet in the name of beer, the conversation all too often turns to the ancient question of which ingredient is the most important.

"Water!" someone will exclaim, citing the nuances of hard versus soft and sulfate levels. Another will invariably argue for malt and another for hops, each extolling the merits of European-grown as opposed to American-grown varieties.

It may seem obvious even to the casual observer that this question is just another version of that classic conundrum: Which of your internal organs is the most important? But a clear case could be made for yeast as the ingredient that has the most direct impact on the flavor of the final beer.

Give me five different yeasts, and I will produce five different beers from the same wort. Imagine using a Belgian abbey strain, a German wheat beer strain, a Munich lager strain, an English ale strain, and a *lambic* culture on the same wort! Would any two of the resulting beers be remotely similar? The brewer's choice of yeast is of paramount importance to the final character of the beer. And, as with malt and hops, British is the way to go when selecting yeast for a mild ale.

A number of very good, readily available British ale yeast strains have been extensively researched and written about, so finding a quality source should not be a problem. Select a moderately attenuative strain, being careful not to let the ale become too dry, as this can rob your beer of character. Because of the relatively low gravity of most mild ales, even mid to highly flocculant strains should do well.

In my experience, the Wyeast London III strain is one of the best for open fermentation. It lends itself well to malty beers, accentuating them with very pleasant bready notes. If you have access to relatively cool—up to 65 °F (18 °C)—fermentation temperatures, another great strain is Wyeast Scotch Ale #1728. Of course, #1056 is always a safe choice. It is very neutral and lets the qualities of the specific ingredients used really come through. Wyeast #1028 is very British in character, but it can easily produce unwanted diacetyl. In truth, any of the London ale yeast strains will do nicely, as will some of the Scotch ale strains. But be careful with Scotch ale strains; some tend to produce a tremendous amount of fruity esters when fermented at high temperatures.

If you are using the more-traditional open fermentation, you would do well to select a strain that is known to be a true top cropper—that is, one that can easily be harvested from the top of a fermenter.

CHAPTER 4

Brewing Equipment and Methods

Much good ale has been drunk out of pewter tankards, old brown jugs, and silver cups; yea, and quaffed in Odin's ghostly hall from the skulls of enemies, in preparing which, no philo-sophical instrument or mechanical appliance was ever used; the modern brewer, however, would never think of trusting to the rule of thumb, but prefers to confide in the dip of the thermometer.

—Alfred Barnard, *The Noted Breweries of Great Britain and Ireland, Vol. II*

Because mild ale is produced by so many breweries in Britain—and has been throughout the history of the brewing industry—the equipment is not specialized and the techniques used to produce it are common to most traditional British ale breweries. Therefore, this chapter offers a description and analysis of the standard British brewing equipment and methods. Where applicable, those methods are analyzed as they pertain specifically to the production of mild ale.

A six-roller mill from the World War II era. According to the staff at Holden's brewery, the rollers on this mill have not been adjusted for 25 years.

The traditional British brewery is organized so that the entire process flows from the top of the building to the bottom. This system, known as the tower system, is designed to mitigate and limit the need for pumps, which in the past were considered costly, unsanitary, and unreliable.

Equipment

The Mill

In days gone by, the brewer had to be concerned with every aspect of the raw materials as well as those of the brewery and the process. The brewer was often the landlord, if not the actual farmer, of the land where his barley was grown. He malted it and brewed with it on the same premises. Today, a brewer need only to be concerned with the analysis of the raw materials that are purchased; the growing and malting are left to the specialists.

Typical wooden grist hoppers on the uppermost floor of Marston's Victorian tower brewery in Burton-upon-Trent, England.

The grist shaker at Highgate Brewery, known affectionately as the coffin, has been in use continuously since the brewery opened in 1898. Note the wooden legs that act as springs.

The brewer's specialty is brewing, and the process begins on the top floor of the brewery. Typically found in the attic rafters of a tower brewery (or as they are sometimes called, the Victorian tower), the grist mill is fed by a malt silo, by large sacks of malted barley, or by a combination of the two. The whole kernels often pass through a shaker screen to remove any foreign matter—such as shards of metal or clumps of dirt—that may have been delivered from the maltster. The kernels are then sent on to the rollers in the mill, which is usually located in the same room. The four- or six-roller apparatus dumps the milled grain into the grist case located directly below.

The Brew House

The grist case is situated between the floor of the mill room and the ceiling of the mash tun room, directly above the grist hydrator. The hydrator infuses the ground malt

A mash tun at Young's Ram Brewery in London. The conical top is made from stainless steel, but the old mash tun itself is cast iron, with wooden staves for insulation. Also note the manometer directly in front of the vessel.

with hot water, limiting the need for excessive stirring of the mash to remove any dry clumps. It is often of the Steele's masher design, in which a worm-drive archemidian screw mixes the malt with the incoming grist. Other designs include a simple conical "china hat" that spreads the incoming grist and water out in a cone-shaped fan into the mash tun.

The typical British brew house includes a mash tun with a false bottom; a copper kettle (often simply referred to as the copper), perhaps with an internal colandria; a hop back; and a counter-flow heat exchanger. The mash tun is often made of cast iron and clad with wooden staves for insulation. The false bottom is usually made of copper or brass, with 10% of the total area of the plates being per-

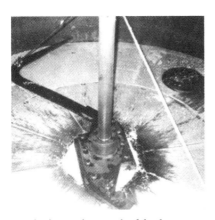

Inside the mash tun. The false bottom is made from copper, with slits no more than 1/32 of an inch in width.

forated. The mash tun frequently has multiple draw-off points, though it is not uncommon to find tuns with a single draw-off point located directly in the center of the vessel.

Especially in older, independent breweries (which most mild ale breweries are), few mash tuns have any sort of automatic spent-grain disposal or even a manway to pull the grains out by hand. In most of these breweries, a man must physically enter the tun after the liquor is drained and remove the spent grains with a shovel, filling buckets by lifting the shovel loads over the side of the vessel. Some breweries also operate without the benefit of mash rakes to facilitate the run-off, although most breweries now have them.

Located on the floor immediately below the mash tun is the brew kettle, or copper, where the collected wort is boiled and hopped. Coppers come in a variety of configurations. Some are large, open copper pots with gas or, in rare cases, coal fires raging beneath; some are covered with nautical-looking copper domes; and others are designed to boil under pressure. All but the most primitive systems are equipped with an internal colandria— an internal tube designed to increase the ratio of heated surface area to wort.

Most brew houses in Britain are not equipped with a whirlpool, but those that are, call it a swirl tank. By far, the more common method of wort clarification is the hop back. Usually little more than a cylindro-conical tank with a screen fitted about halfway down the cone, the hop back uses the screen to catch the hop flowers in the wort, later using them to filter the whole of the wort after the boil. This

These side-by-side coppers at Highgate date from the 1950s. They are nearly identical, but the brewers prefer the one on the left. They say that they get a better boil in that one.

The copper at Holden's Brewery. This vessel is somewhat unique to mild ale breweries, in that it is designed to boil under pressure.

method both clarifies the wort and allows the brewer to add fresh hops for added aroma to the hop back before running the wort through.

Fermentation Systems

> I am a firm advocate for rousing, Light Ale commence 24 hours after pitching, until within 12 hours of skimming or cleansing, Strong Ale 36 hours after pitching, until within 12 hours of skimming or cleansing.
>
> —Professor George Stewart Amsinck
> *Practical Brewings: A Series of Fifty Brewings*

I will briefly discuss several traditional fermentation methods that are commonly used in breweries that produce mild ales. Each system is designed to keep the yeast in suspension and to facilitate harvesting the healthiest and most viable cells after primary fermentation is complete. Whether these systems have produced yeasts of the non-flocculating or highly flocculant type through the process of natural selection or whether the systems themselves were designed around the yeasts available to the brewer can only be a matter of speculation. The common systems of fermentation are characterized by the degree to which they facilitate rousing.

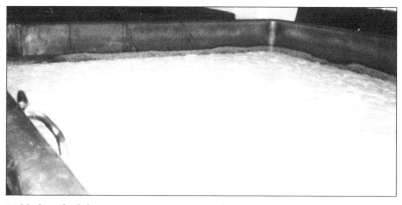

Mild ale at high kraeusen in an open square fermenter.

Open squares or rounds. Fermenting in open squares or rounds is the simplest system of ale fermentation and is the method most commonly used in independent British breweries. It is simply a matter of running the hopped, cooled wort into vessels that are shallow (6 to 13 feet deep), oversized, and open to the air. These vessels are often made of wood (oak, fir, and American cedar are favored), with the rounds fastened by iron hoops, as is common with barrels. The squares are usually made of planks up to 2 inches thick that are either fitted together by a carpenter with dovetails joints or held in place by nuts and bolts. Both rounds and squares were traditionally coated with pitch or varnish. Nowadays, the old vessels are more likely to be lined with stainless steel or plastic.

A sufficient quantity of yeast is pitched into the wort, and fermentation begins. In the deeper cylindrical and cylindro-conical vessels, where there is a low volume-to-surface-area ratio, the yeast works up very little top-crop and is mainly harvested at the base. In these shallow, open fermenters, the yeast rises to the top of the beer after fermentation and is harvested from there.

The philosophy of fermentation divides into two camps at this point—the skimmers and droppers. The

Open wooden rounds. These vessels date from the early twentieth century; they are now lined with UHMW plastic.

Open stainless-steel fermenters of both square and round design at Holden's.

skimming system is the oldest and most basic method of conducting fermentation. Its has its roots in a time when all yeast was considered to be an objectionable by-product of fermentation and was therefore discarded. In this system, the entire fermentation and maturation is done in a single vessel.

After primary fermentation has begun and the yeast is at high kraeusen—that is, the most viable yeast is at the height of its activity, and a thick, rocky or cauliflower-like head has formed on the wort—the yeast is removed from the top by sliding a long board across the whole surface of the vessel within a few inches of the liquid beneath the head.

The yeast is skimmed every 10 to 12 hours. The first skimming, contaminated by albumin, hop resins, and the most unattenuative yeast, is discarded, as is the last, which is often full of dead or mutating yeast cells. The middle skimmings, which contain the youngest, healthiest, most attenuative cells, are collected in a yeast back

Open oaken squares at Highgate. These vessels were lined with stainless steel in 1995.

and stored, usually open to the air, at a cool temperature or refrigerated until needed for pitching. The skimming is continued until the brewer judges that the fermentation has just enough strength to throw up one more thin head to act as a barrier to the ambient air for the short maturation period.

The skimming system is equally effective with flocculant and nonflocculant yeast strains. Often, when using the former, a brewer will elect to rouse the yeast directly after skimming. Before the 1940s, this was frequently done by dropping a tethered bucket pierced with hundreds of holes into the wort, letting it sink, and then pulling it up from the bottom several times. Today it is standard practice to employ an immersible pump to keep the yeast in suspension.

Any variation of the skimming system in which the wort is run down into a second vessel for yeast harvesting is known as a cleansing system. The simplest method of cleansing is the dropping system, in which the fermenting wort is run into vessels of the same general description as the first—that is, from one 50-barrel round into another 50-barrel round. The goal is to leave behind most of the sediment (made up of hop particulates and cold break), as well as the hop resins and dead yeast cells that make up a significant portion of the first head on fermenting wort. Dropping serves to mix and further aerate the wort, virtually eliminating the need for rousing, except in the case of a few breweries that must rouse anyway because of the highly flocculent nature of their yeast.

In some breweries, dropping is done at 24 hours into fermentation; in others, it is done when the wort gravity has dropped halfway to the expected final value. That is, when it is at high kreusen, and the temperature has reached its maximum.

Burton Unions. The Burton Unions constitute the rarest system of fermentation in Britain, with only one traditional brewery still using it and only one American microbrewery using a variation of it. Although once widely used, especially among the pale ale breweries of Burton-on-Trent, the unions have been replaced by more efficient and more cost-effective methods by all but Marston, Thompson, and Evershed of Pedigree Bitter fame.

Marston's produces two beers known as milds, each of which is a member of their Brewer's Choice line of specialty products and, as such, are some of the only beers produced *entirely* in the union system. (Marston's other products, including Pedigree Bitter, are blended beers, and unlike the Head Brewer's Choice beers, are made up of only a small percentage of beer fermented in the unions blended with a large amount of beer fermented in stainless steel open fermenters.)

The union system is an ancestor of the oldest fermentation methods, in which the beers were fermented entirely in the casks from which they would eventually be served, or they were cleansed in these casks after primary fermentation in larger vessels. This ancient method of fermentation is still used in some very small, artisanal breweries in Belgium, but it has gone entirely out of use in the rest of the world. Known as fermentation in loose pieces,

the approach was effective when brewing was a cottage industry, but it is far too wasteful, time-consuming, and expensive for use in larger breweries. Those constraints led brewers to develop a more effective variation.

In the Burton Union System, the wort is initially pitched in a large, open tun and allowed to begin fermenting. Just as the first signs of a yeast head begin to appear (after 5 to 15 hours)

The Old Union Room at Marston's in Burton-on-Trent.

the wort is dropped into the union sets. These sets consist of a number of 4-barrel casks, usually in two rows of 12 casks, fitted on a stillage (or trunnion), underneath a long trough called a barm back or a top trough. The bung holes on the bulge of the casks are fitted swan necks that empty into the barm back, as

FIGURE 1

Diagram of the Burton Union System

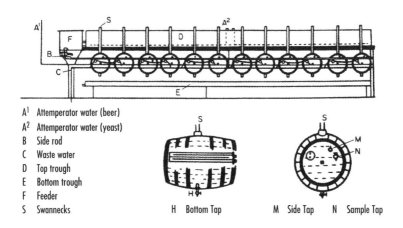

A[1]	Attemperator water (beer)
A[2]	Attemperator water (yeast)
B	Side rod
C	Waste water
D	Top trough
E	Bottom trough
F	Feeder
S	Swannecks

H   Bottom Tap

M   Side Tap   N   Sample Tap

shown in figure 1. The top trough is kept at a cooler temperature than the unions to facilitate sedimentation of the yeast. The trough is slightly tilted to one end, where several holes at different levels allow the beer to flow into a second back, called a feeder, which in turn directs the flow back to the casks via the side rods. Each cask is fitted with an attemperator, as is the barm back and the feeder.

This method is most effective when used with a non-flocculant strain of yeast. There is no need to rouse the wort, as the yeast will remain in suspension naturally. In fact, the purpose of the barm back, in addition to providing a place from which to harvest yeast, is to facilitate the cleansing of the beer.

During early fermentation (the first 5 to 15 hours in the union), the wort is allowed to flow back into the casks via the lowest hole in the barm back. This permits the maximum amount of yeast to remain in the bulk of the fermenting beer. During the middle of fermentation (15 to 36 hours), the wort flows through a hole just above the sedimented yeast in the back, ensuring that only clear product flows back into the casks.

Unions at high kraeusen. Note the foam spewing from the swan necks atop the wooden casks.

This system is so effective as to render the beer virtually bright as it is dropped through valves in the bottom
of the casks into a racking tun. From there, the beer will
be racked into the trade casks.

Yorkshire stone squares. Among the rarer methods of
fermentation, the Yorkshire stone squares are designed
to keep the highly flocculant yeast strains typically used
in Yorkshire and Lancashire breweries in suspension.
The system is characterized by the relatively small capacity of the fermenting vessels (50 barrels or less). It consists of a fermenting square surmounted by a barm back
with a manhole cut in the center of the separating deck
(see figure 2). This manhole is generally about 18 inches
in diameter and surrounded by a lip 5 or 6 inches high.

The deck is also pierced by up to three additional
holes. The first is usually fitted with a long, stainless steel
or copper "organ pipe" that reaches nearly to the bottom
of the lower square. The second pipe is fitted with a pump
to transfer fermenting wort to the top square, and the
third serves as a drain for the top square. The vessels are
traditionally made of impervious stone or slate, as is the
case at the most famous stone-square brewery, Samuel
Smith's of Tadcaster. Temperature control was originally

achieved by means of a water jacket, but today it is now exclusively managed by means of an attemperator.

Historically, yeast was mixed with the wort in the upper square and allowed to run into the lower square via the manhole. This falling action sufficiently aerating the wort. In modern breweries, the wort is first run into an open vessel, where it is pitched with a highly flocculant yeast strain before being dropped almost immediately into the Yorkshire squares. The action of fermentation forces the yeast head through the manhole and into the top square, where the run-off back into the bottom square via the organ pipe is regulated with a valve.

FIGURE 2

Diagram of the Yorkshire Stone Square System

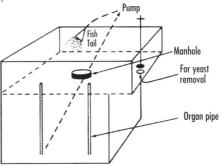

Between 20 and 30 hours after pitching, the brewer begins to pump the fermenting wort from the lower to the upper squares before allowing it to run back into the lower square. This action is designed to keep the yeast in suspension and to attain proper attenuation. This pumping typically occurs for periods of 5 to 10 minutes every 4 to 6 hours until the proper degree of attenuation is achieved. When the fermentation is almost complete, the valve into the bottom square is closed, and the remaining yeast is harvested for repitching.

Because of the highly flocculant nature of the yeast and the almost continuous pumping that is required to facilitate attenuation, these beers often exhibit a pronounced diacetyl character. That is not objectionable in lower concentrations in some bitters and pale ales, but it is not part of the typical modern mild ale profile.

The Burton Union and the Yorkshire stone square systems would probably have been completely abandoned due to the labor and waste involved if it were not for the fact that they have special claims with respect to the quality and character of the beers produced in them. The cost of the union system is so prohibitively high that all save one brewery has discontinued their use and only a few remain true to the squares. As it is, only a very few brewers continue to use them.

Dual-stage closed fermentation. A very common method of fermentation in modern ale breweries and the most common form among homebrewers is closed dual-stage fermentation. Closed fermentation allows for greater sanitation and retention of more CO_2 than open fermentation. The process entails pitching yeast into one vessel and then transferring the cooled wort on top of it.

The temperature is controlled by glycol- or water-filled jackets surrounding the tanks or, in the case of home-brewing, by the ambient temperature. Fermentation is allowed to continue until complete attenuation has been achieved. The beer is then typically allowed to sit at fermentaion temperature for another 24 hours.

At the end of this period, which is intended to give the yeast time to reabsorb and metabolize the undesirable by-products of fermentation, the temperature is dropped to around 50 °F (10 °C) to encourage flocculation. The beer is then transferred off the yeast sediment and into another vessel of the same or similar design for cold maturation. Last, it is either racked into trade casks, bottled, or filtered and kegged.

Uni-tank or cylindro-conical fermentation. Developed by the Rainier Brewing Company in the 1940s, the uni-tank system is by far the most common method adopted by American microbreweries, as well as by many larger breweries. The advantage of this system is that the same closed vessel can be used for primary and secondary fermentation as well as for lagering. The system is comprised of a tall, cylindrical tank with a conical bottom. Although earlier tanks had cones as shallow as 25° from horizontal, modern research suggests that an angle of 70° is optimal.

The uni-tank system is quite similar to dual-stage fermentation, with the important difference being that there is no transfer after primary fermentation. As the beer in the tank is cooled, the flocculating yeast fills the cone and becomes quite compact, which makes it easy to harvest and drain excess yeast from the bottom of the cone. By the end of this process, the beer is relatively free of yeast.

However, not all yeasts flocculate well. That means that there can be a significant possibility that not all of the yeast will not be removed through the bottom of the cone. This is especially true if there are any ledges inside the fermenter, such as those often found around a manway or a temperature probe. This excess yeast remaining in the beer may produce off-flavors due to autolysis of the yeast during extended maturation.

Grundy tanks. The American craftbrewing industry has always been characterized by the innovation of its members. Dairy tanks, being more affordable than new tanks, were often pressed into service for anything from brew house vessels to fermenters to serving tanks in a brewpub.

One other tank has gained such popularity both in America and abroad that it deserves mention here as common brewery equipment. The Grundy Company of Great Britain manufactured tanks for the growing bulk beer market in the 1960s, 1970s, and early 1980s. The tanks,

A Grundy tank. This tank is converted for use as a serving tank in the cellar of Quarry Ridge Brewery in Berea, Ohio.

holding either 90 U.K. gallons or 220 U.K. gallons, were installed in the cellars of pubs, which were rapidly moving away from selling real ale. The breweries then filled tanker trucks with their filtered, carbonated product and these trucks filled the Grundy tanks.

With the growth of the craftbrewing movement in the United Kingdom, Grundy tanks fell from use as receptacles for bulk beers and became useful to small breweries for a variety of uses. Sarah Hughes's brewery in Sedgely, brewers of the famous Dark Ruby Mild, use converted Grundy tanks for open fermenters while scores of American brewers use them for various tasks including hot and cold liquor tanks and serving vessels.

Fermentation in the home brewery. The information provided in this section should give you a good sense of the main methods of fermentation used in mild ale breweries today. As interesting as these methods are, though, the fact is that brewers—small or large—tend to ferment in whatever they have at hand. Small breweries are limited to the tanks already in place; they must select temperature curves and yeast strains with these vessels in mind.

Very few small breweries can afford the luxury of tailoring their equipment to the beers they intend to make. The ones that can afford to do so are breweries that have decidedly special circumstances. For example, the Firestone-Walker Brewery in Los Olivos, California, uses 60-gallon oak barrels set up much like the Burton Union to ferment their Double Barrel Ale. The typical homebrewer has very few options, for it is unlikely that he or she will opt to undertake the extreme measure of replicating Yorkshire squares or Burton Unions in the livingroom or garage.

Most homebrewing texts describe in detail how to use a closed plastic bucket or a glass carboy with an airlock as a fermenter. This method works well for mild ales. Because of the relative low gravity of modern mild ales, it is easy to turn out a completely fermented batch in very little time.

The Brewing Process

As one might expect, in terms of equipment and procedures, brewing mild ale is very much the same as brewing any other sort of British ale. What is different is the extra vigilance required to keep beers of such modest strength fresh and clean throughout fermentation and beyond. Some of these beers, especially the modern interpretations of the style, have such a delicate flavor profile that even the lowest levels of off-flavors can be very noticeable and unpleasant. Almost neurotic attention must be paid to cleanliness and gentleness throughout the brewing process.

Grinding the Malt

I prefer grinding low than otherwise, there need be no fear of bad draining from the mash tun, if the malt is made as above, and the first liquor

not taken to high, a great deal of extract is sac-
rificed from grinding too high, merely for the
purpose of ensuring safe spending, one tap is
quite sufficient in the tun.

—George Stewart Amsinck
Practical Brewings: A Series of Fifty Brewings

If all the mild ale brewer were concerned with during
mashing were the extraction and conversion of starches
into sugars through the simple act of infusing the malt
with hot water, then grinding the malt into flour would be
universally accepted as the method of choice. But finely
ground malt particles would form a dense, water-tight
cake in the mash tun, that would make any sort of filtration and run-off prohibitively slow, if not impossible. If
the grains are ground too coarsely, or not at all, too much
of the starchy interior of the malt kernel would be left
unconverted and unrecoverable.

Malt should be ground so that the husks, for the most
part, remain unshredded—cracked open just enough for
the maximum amount of the starchy endosperm to be
exposed to the hot water of the mash. The malt must
remain intact enough for the grain-bed of the mash to be
airy, and porous enough for the wort and sparge water to
easily trickle through it. It must be tight enough to act as

a filter bed that will trap the unwanted proteins and particulate before the wort enters the copper to be boiled.

In order to achieve this goal with the typical two-, four-, or six-roller malt mill, the malt must be of high quality— well modified and very dry. High-quality malt is of uniform size and modification. It stands to reason that one can only mill malt to equal quality if it is already of equal kernel size. Malted barley that is not uniform in size and color cannot be evenly modified and kilned. The hard, granular grits in a poorly modified malt will tend to adhere to the husks and therefore be unavailable for conversion.

If the malt is slack—that is, becoming stale because of exposure to moisture—the malt will tend to stick to the rollers during milling and, at worst, gum up the rolls or, at best, compress and fail to crack. Either way, the results will be unsatisfactory. Some of the malt will merely squeeze between the rolls instead of cracking as it passes through. Before malt mills became as advanced as they are today, it was common practice to lightly sprinkle the malt with water before milling; some brewers still do it. The water leaves the interior of the malt brittle, while giving the husks some elasticity, making it less likely that the malt will shred during milling.

The ideal mild ale grist is composed of 75% grits, 18% husks, and 7% flour. A grist composed of more than 9 or

10% flour is likely to yield poor extract, and it may even lend an unfilterable haze to the finished beer. The excess flour balls up during the mash, isolating a significant amount of the convertible starch from the enzymes responsible for conversion. If any of this starch makes its way into the kettle during sparging, the beer will have some degree of protein haze.

It is best to brew with your malt as soon as possible after it is ground. The flour and grits are very hygroscopic and will absorb any available moisture. And that can turn your malt grist into an ideal growing medium for acid-producing bacteria.

If you wish, you can test the breakdown of your grist with a set of malt screens, which can be purchased from one of several professional brewery suppliers. The screens generally consist of five or six standard mesh-bottomed dishes of decreasing coarseness. However, the screens are quite expensive. Unless you are able to befriend a professional brewer and borrow the screens as needed, you might be better off with a simple visual inspection followed by empirical observation.

In any case, it makes sense to keep track of the yield you get from your malt to be used as an indicator of how good your crush is for your particular arrangement.

Doughing In

> A mashing machine is of great advantage to the
> modern brewer, as by its use, the mass becomes
> uniform in consistency, and the goods are less
> liable to be converted into a paste, from which
> the impregnated water could not be separated.
>
> —Alfred Barnard, *The Noted*
> *Breweries of Great Britain and Ireland, Vol. II*

A large brew house capable of producing thousands of barrels per year, circa 1764.

> The correct heat in the first wetting the malt, stamps the character of the whole gyle, the heat most adapted to open the pores of the grain must be correct, and after that is done, a higher heat can be added, without prejudice to the flavour of the Wort, a rich flavour of the Malt, is what we seek to obtain in the Beer.
>
> —George Stewart Amsinck
> *Practical Brewings: A Series of Fifty Brewings*

Professional brewers of mild ale typically use some sort of grain hydrator as they mix hot water and malt for the mash. In British breweries, it is not uncommon to find a Victorian device known as a Steele's masher mounted above the mash tun. A Steele's masher takes the grist and sends it through a cylinder by means of an archemedian screw. At this point, hot water is added and mixed with the grist as it travels down the cylinder and drops into the tun below.

In smaller breweries and homebreweries, the tun is simply filled with water at the appropriate strike temperature and the grist is dumped into it. The brewer then stirs the mash with a paddle until no dry spots remain. It is important to remember that, when employing the single-temperature infusion method, the strike temperature has to be higher than the conversion temperature you are aiming for. That is because you are mixing a huge quantity of malt with water that is at a much lower temperature, which will push the overall mash temperature down. In my brewery, the strike temperature needs to be about 16–20 °F (9–11 °C) above the required mash temperature, depending upon the temperature of the malt. (We have to raise our strike temperature a little more in the winter because we store the malt in a cold warehouse.)

Stirring the mash. The absence of a mechanized apparatus necessitates the laborious task of stirring with a canoe paddle.

The Mash

The first process in brewing is just like making tea on a gigantic scale, the copper being the tea kettle, the mash tun the teapot. The proper degree of heat of the water with which the crushed or bruised malt is mashed is of the utmost consequence. Too cold, it would fail to

extract the virtues of the malt; too hot, the
whole would be apt to run into a sort of starch.
—Alfred Barnard, *The Noted Breweries of*
Great Britain and Ireland, Vol. II

As with most beers made from well-modified British-style malts, the optimum method for brewing mild ale as it existed three hundred years ago—or as it exists today—is the single-temperature infusion mash. Because the temperature at mash-in is the temperature at which we convert, there is no mixing required and, therefore, no further shredding of the malt and husks.

The proper conversion temperature for brewing a mild ale is a highly debatable question. Most of the commercial breweries willing to share such information report that their typical mash temperature is between 151 and 155 °F (66 and 68 °C), with one noteworthy exception—Highgate and Walsall mashes their dark mild at 158 °F (70 °C). The lower end of this range yields more fermentable sugars and will finish drier, with a higher alcohol content; the higher end will produce fewer fermentable sugars and more unfermentable dextrins, resulting in a final product with more body and mouthfeel and less alcohol.

For the well-modified, batch-consistent pale malts available from British maltsters today, complete starch

Iodine Test for Starch Conversion

The simplest way to know whether all of the starches available for conversion in your mash have indeed converted into sugar and dextrins is to use tincture of iodine as an indicator. Iodine will turn starch granules a very dark purple color; if all of the starches in your mash have converted, the iodine will not change color.

To perform the test, take a small amount of liquid from your mash (about one tablespoon or so) and place it on a piece of white glazed porcelain (a tile square or a saucer). Be certain that there are no actual grains in the sample, as the starches in the husks will invariably turn purple and invalidate the test. Place a small drop of iodine in the mash liquid and observe. If the iodine turns purple or black, you should continue mashing at the conversion temperature. Redo the test every few minutes until you obtain negative results.

conversion can take place within 45 minutes and is almost certainly complete after one hour at the conversion temperature. A simple iodine test will reveal how long to allow for complete starch conversion in your brewery. The test takes only a minute or so and is well worth the effort until you get to know the malt you are working with.

Recirculation

After conversion has taken place, a significant portion of the mash liquid must be drawn off the bottom of the mash tun and placed back on top of the mash. The idea here is to use the settled mash as its own filter bed, removing particulate that has slipped through the false bottom and putting it on top of the grain bed so that the particles get caught up and the wort runs clear. This process is crucial in mild ale brewing, as the off-flavors that can arise if too many grain husks make it into the boil will be especially objectionable in these low-gravity beers.

This process must be done gently. The wort must be drawn off the bottom very slowly to avoid setting the grain bed, and it must be reintroduced at the top without causing a hole to be drilled into the mash and without creating too much aeration. Most professional breweries have diffusers of some sort built into the mash tun for this purpose, but homebrewers can achieve the same results by placing a small saucer on top of the mash and pouring the wort onto it as a diffuser.

The recirculation should last as long as necessary to ensure as bright a wort as possible, without compromising the mash temperature. Most professional breweries have well-insulated mash tuns, but unless you are mashing into a cooler at home, it is likely that your mash will cool off rather rapidly. Don't feel that you are being too neurotic if you find yourself putting an old blanket around the mash tun while you are recirculating in order to keep from losing too much heat. Once the wort is sufficiently clear, you are ready to begin running off into the kettle.

Run-off and Sparge

Because of the relatively small mash required for brewing a mild ale, it is tempting to run off too quickly. Although compacting, or setting, the bed is not as likely as it is when producing a higher-gravity beer, it can become a problem when brewing a mild ale if any adjunctive grains like oats, corn, or wheat have been used. Even if there are no adjuncts and the mash is light and airy, and there is no risk of setting the bed, running-off too quickly will result in a poor yield.

The run-off of first wort should continue until the top of the grain bed is visible through a very thin layer of wort. At this point, the brewer should begin to sparge with hot water. Sparging—the process of washing the last extractives from the mash—is generally performed by sprinkling water hotter than the mash (up to 176 °F or 80 °C) over the top of the grain bed and allowing it to trickle through. This will leach the last sugars from the grain.

I have personally achieved outstanding results by sparging with water at or only slightly above the conversion temperature, both in professional brewing environments and as a homebrewer. There are many advantages to this lower-temperature approach. It requires less hot liquor, but more importantly, there is less risk of leaching unwanted tannins and silicates from the grains; the former produces objectionable off-flavors, and the latter can cause an irreversible haze. It allows enzymatic activity to continue throughout the sparging and run-off time, which can help complete starch conversions that may not have occurred in some small pockets of the mash. In addition, lower-temperature sparging tends to decrease the chances of leaching unwanted silicates, tannins, phosphates, and unfermentable polysaccharides from the grains. These compounds will impart undesirable flavors and aromas either in and of themselves, or as precursors to an objectionable flavor.

In theory, lower-temperature sparges are supposed to reduce your brew house yield by failing to solubilize all available sugars. However, I have found this loss to be so minimal as to be merely academic. The benefits, in my opinion, vastly outweigh the minuscule loss of yield.

This practice is a very good way to save your mild ale—in particular, pale milds, with their delicate aromas and flavors—from being too harsh in tannic astringency. In fact, I can find no reason, either practical or theoretical, not to extend this practice to the brewing of all other styles of beer, except where the elevated temperature might mitigate slow run-off in very high-gravity beers such as barley wine, old ale, and imperial stout. (However, in these cases, the flavor profile is so intense that any off-flavors resulting from a sparge that is too hot will be easily masked.)

If you decide to disregard everything I have said about the brewing process up to this point, please heed this single axiom of mild ale brewing: DO **NOT** OVER-SPARGE!

One sure way to dissolve a detectable amount of tannins and silicates is to run wort of too-low a gravity into your kettle and boil it. Stop collecting wort when the specific gravity of the run-off reaches 1.012 (3 °P). Collecting more will only slightly increase your yield, but it will most assuredly lend your mild an unfilterable and unfinable haze, as well as an unwanted tannic astringency.

Boiling and Hopping

With only a few very esoteric styles of beer excepted, a properly conducted boil is essential to the brewing of all styles of beer. A vigorous, consistently maintained, and lengthy boil can very well make the difference between a world-class beer and a mediocre beer. Boiling destroys all the enzymes that are left over from the mash, in addition to stabilizing and sterilizing the wort. It extracts hop resins and isomerizes bittering alpha acids, concentrates the wort, coagulates and precipitates unwanted proteins, and lowers the wort pH for optimal fermentation. It also drives off harsh hop oils and off-flavor precursors like dimethyl sulfoxide (DMSO), which leads to dimethyl sulfide (DMS)—the signature cooked corn flavor found in Rolling Rock, which is *not* desirable in mild ale.

Boiling can commence as soon as the first wort covers the heated surface. In the case of direct-fired gas kettles, this is as soon as the wort fully covers the surface that is in contact with the flame. For steam-jacketed kettles, this is as soon as the wort covers the bottom steam jacket (if that jacket can be isolated). It is important to observe these details. There will be significant color pick-up and caramelization of sugars if the wort is allowed to sit against the heated surface and burn. This is actually desirable for some styles of beer (namely Scotch ale), and it might be an interesting exercise in a mild ale, but heating your kettle without any liquid in it is ill-advised because it tends to weaken the metal. This is especially true of direct-fired kettles where the temperature of the fire far exceeds the 230 °F (110 °C) that is common with steam.

The rate at which water evaporates from your wort is important in brewing mild ale because of the relatively delicate flavor profile of milds. In addition, the evaporation rate is indicative of the efficiency of the boil and how much of the off-flavor precursors and volatile hop oils, ketones, and sulfur compounds are being driven off. A rate of 10% evaporation per hour of boil is standard in the brewing industry. Anything more is gravy; anything less is inadequate.

A rolling, vigorous boil must be maintained for a minimum of 90 minutes. Isomerization, coagulation, and precipitation are not solely temperature-dependent—they also depend on agitation. At least 60 minutes of the boil should take place with the bittering hops. Extended boils of three hours or more will adversely affect hop utilization and tend to disassociate the coagulated proteins.

The pH of the wort at the beginning of the boil should fall between 5.2 and 5.5. A pH of 5.2 is best for protein coagulation and precipitation; a slightly more basic pH is best for hop utilization. In most cases, the transition to the more basic pH happens naturally due to the acidity of the brewing water, the additional acidification that comes from the use of dark malts, enzymatic activity, and the application of heat. If corrections need to be made, a food-grade phosphoric acid or calcium carbonate (gypsum) can be added directly to the kettle.

Bittering hops. The bittering compounds in hops, known as alpha acids, are not very water-soluble; they must be molecularly altered or isomerized during the boil in order for them to stay in suspension. Isomerization is dependent on both the heat of the boil and the rolling motion of the mixture. A hot but placid boil will adversely affect hop utilization. Even the most efficient kettles can only be expected to eke no more than 38% utilization out of the alpha acids added to the boil; in most homebrew environments, less than 33% utilization is common (assuming the brewer is using pelletized hops—utilization will be somewhat less if whole hop flowers are used).

A significant portion of the iso-alpha-acids in the wort will be lost during fermentation. Some of them are lost on the sides of the fermenter in the foam residue, and more are absorbed by the yeast and then lost when the yeast falls out of suspension or gets filtered out. This kind of loss represents about 3% of the total alpha acid added to the kettle, bringing the apparent utilization as measured in the finished product down to no more than 35% for commercial brewers and 30% for homebrewers.

Typically, British brewers add their hops (almost invariably as whole hop flowers) just as the wort comes to a boil. The boil lasts for no more than 90 minutes and sometimes as little as 60 minutes. When I worked at John Harvard's Brew House in Cleveland, Ohio, we almost invariably boiled the wort for 2 hours. The extended boil didn't hurt the clarity of the wort, and we had great results with the quality of the finished product. Also, it has been demonstrated that some of the iso-alpha acids are lost if you add hops before the first hot break is formed because the acids precipitate with the proteins.

Late hopping. Most British brewers add hops at least twice during the boil, and some add hops up to four different times. The theory is that hops added during the last 10–20 minutes of the boil will impart more of the aromatic character of the hops because less of those oils are driven off during the boil. Hops that are added for the last half hour will impart more hop flavor than aroma and, of course, hops added to the hop back or directly to the fermented beer will impart aroma very similar to the aroma of the hop flower itself.

The hop back and whirlpool. After the boil is complete, the bitter wort must be clarified of all the unwanted coagulated protein that we precipitated during the boil and the hop particulate, whether in the form of whole hop flowers or the fine dust of hydrated hop pellets. In a traditional British brewery, this would be done almost exclusively with a hop back. As mentioned earlier, the hop back usually takes the form of a cone-bottomed tank with a screen fitted in the cone.

The brewer has the option of adding late hop aroma by putting fresh hop flowers on the screen and running all the boiled bitter wort through them. The screens, any hops the brewer puts on them, and the hops that get

Inside a hop back.

caught as the wort passes through help clarify the beer by acting as a filter bed, much like the mash did during recirculation. The filter bed removes all the unwanted hot break—the proteins leached from the malt and precipitated and coagulated during the boil. Many British brewers swear that the hop character they get from adding fresh hops to the hop back is unlike the character they get by late kettle-hopping or dry-hopping during fermentation or in the cask.

Most breweries in the United States are not equipped with specialized equipment for use as a hop back. However, several of John Harvard's Brew Houses (as well as Commonwealth Brewing in Boston, Massachusetts, and some others) use the mash tun—which by this point in the process has been cleared of spent grains and cleaned—as a hop back. The surface area of the screens is, admittedly, a lot larger than a typical hop back for the system would be, but the effect is about the same.

Hot-side aeration is an issue when using any hop back, but I have found no British breweries that are concerned about aeration of the hot wort; after all, their beers get packaged and consumed within a few weeks of leaving the cellars. Hot-side aeration is mainly an issue when the beer in question is intended to be packaged as a filtered, bottled product that may sit on retail shelves for extended periods before consumption. Hot-side aeration produces precursors to staling compounds and, over time, will impart to the beer oxidized flavors and aromas.

At home, a large strainer or colander that fits inside of a pot can be used, or better yet, a perforated clam steamer. Place some fresh hop cones in the colander and slowly pour the wort through. In most American breweries, especially the smaller ones, the prevailing method of wort clarification is the whirlpool tank, first developed by Molson Breweries of Canada. The whirlpool comprises a vertical cylindrical tank into which the wort is pumped at a fairly high velocity at a tangential angle, causing the hot wort to swirl into a vortex. The result, much like mixing sugar in a glass of iced tea, where the undissolved sugar collects in a cone in the center of the glass, is a pile of separated hot trub in the center of the whirlpool.

After wort clarification, the wort is cooled by means of a counterflow chiller. There, cold water passes in the opposite direction past the hot wort, and a temperature gradient is formed that allows the heat to be exchanged. The wort comes out cool, and the water comes out hot— usually to be recovered and used in the process of the next brew. Historically, the wort was cooled by other means, the most ancient of which was the cool-ship, which is still used in many Belgian breweries and a very few British breweries, including Traquair House in the Scottish Borders.

The cool-ship is a shallow vessel designed to increase the surface area of the wort that is exposed to the air. This vessel was also used as a method of hop separation; the vessel acted as a sedimentation tank, with the clear wort being run off the top and the precipitated proteins and hops left at the bottom. This is a very inefficient method, though, and the ratio of lost wort to recovered wort is dramatic.

Fermentation

> Pitching is an important part, as far as Yeast is concerned, the Yeast from a Gyle brewed on Monday, and cleansed or skimmed on the Wednesday would be in condition for pitching on Saturday or Monday following, and no longer, and in summer stop at Saturday, drain off the beer as solid as possible, on the same day, that it is intended to be made use of, the wort should be pitched at the same heat you intend the Gyle to be.
>
> —George Stewart Amsinck
> *Practical Brewings: A Series of Fifty Brewings*

Attemporators in an open, stainless-steel square fermenter at Young's Ram Brewery in London. Cool glycol or, in some cases, water flows through the attemporators to control the fermentation temperature.

The nature of fermentation was not understood until Pasteur developed his theory of fermentation and devised the principles of sanitation, sterilization, and a technique for culturing microorganisms. Yeast and its role in the brewing process was so misunderstood that for most of history, it was regarded as a detrimental scum that should be disposed of as quickly as possible. By the middle of the seventeenth century, some brewers were repitching yeast and beating the kraeusen back into

TABLE 2

Average Pitching Rates and Temperatures
(lbs. thick slurry to the imperial barrel)

Wort Gravity	Pitching Rate	Pitching Temp.	Maximum Temp.	Racking Temp.
1.030	0.66 lbs.	60 °F (15.5 °C)	66 °F (19 °C)	53–54 °F (11.5–12 °C)
1.040	0.75 lbs.	59 °F (15 °C)	67 °F (19.5 °C)	" "
1.050	1.50 lbs.	58 °F (14.5 °C)	68 °F (20 °C)	" "
1.060	2.00 lbs.	57 °F (14 °C)	69 °F (20.5 °C)	" "
1.080	2–3.00 lbs.	57 °F (14 °C)	70 °F (21 °C)	" "

the fermenting beer, although they didn't understand the science behind this practice.

During the last century significant strides have been ·made in understanding fermentation and yeast metabolism. The factors that affect fermentation—the particular strain of yeast and its characteristics, the amount of yeast pitched, the aeration of the wort, and fermentation temperature—have been isolated and studied. The result has been the development of better and more economical systems of fermentation.

Primary fermentation. In traditional independent British breweries, the fermentation temperature for mild ale is either ambient (during cooler months), controlled by water-cooled attemperators immersed in the fermenting wort or, more rarely, controlled by a water-filled jacket around the vessel. British brewers typically use higher fermentation temperatures for lower-gravity beers, employing temperatures at pitching of upwards of 60 °F (15.5 °C) for low-gravity beers and as low as 57 °F (14 °C) for higher-gravity beers (see table 2).

Disunited unions. Each cask in the unions is taken out of the line and replaced with another on a regular schedule for reconditioning.

In terms of cell count, British breweries are all over the board. A few mild ale brewers (two for certain) use no method other than pitching roughly one-quarter of the yeast harvested from the previous brew. For British ales of all types, though, the popular British brewing text *Malting and Brewing Science* recommends eight 16×10^6 cells/ml. There is a lot of variation among breweries, but as a general rule, the rate of attenuation and temperature rise occurs at about a decrease of 1 degree of specific gravity (.26 °P) for every 2 hours or 12 degrees (3.07 °P) a day, and a rise of 1 °F every 8 hours (1.75 °C every 24 hours). The temperature is allowed to rise at its own pace for about 36 hours.

At this point, the brewer checks the temperature every 4 to 6 hours until fermentation temperature is reached. After one full day at fermentation temperature, the yeast is harvested, and the temperature is maintained for 6 to 12 hours thereafter. The beer is then gradually cooled to racking temperature at a rate of 1 °F (.6 °C) every 4 to 6 hours. In all cases, "crash cooling" is avoided to ensure that the fermentation cycle is complete and that the yeast has time and the proper environment to scavenge any off-flavor precursors present as by-products of fermentation.

Secondary fermentation. When there is only 1% or less fermentable sugar left, the beer is moved from the primary fermenter into a secondary fermenter, where it is typically cooled to 50 °F (10 °C) or so to begin flocculating the remaining yeast and to prevent any invading microorganisms that may have gotten into the beer from spoiling it. The beer is allowed to rest while the final bit of fermentation takes place, free of the sediment of primary fermentation that might impair the flavor due to autolyzing yeast.

Cleaning the Brewery

> In short, the Reason why Publick and Common
> Brewers seldom or never Brew good Drink is,
> That they . . . Brew so often, that they cannot

sufficiently, between one Brewing and another,
cleanse and scald their brewing Vessels and Barrels, giving them due time to dry, but that they
will retain such a Rest as will always Char and
Sour their Liquors.

—Richard Bradley
A Guide to Gentleman Farmers and
Housekeepers for Brewing the Finest Malt Liquors

The brewing process creates quite a bit of excess material that must be completely removed from the brewing
equipment before it is used again. Everything from spent
grain in the mash tun to beerstone in the copper or yeast
deposits on fermentation vessels must be cleared away,
and all the equipment should be cleaned and sanitized
between each brewing session. Large, modern breweries—and a great number of smaller ones—use a variety
of chemicals to accomplish these tasks. Strong alkalis like
sodium hydroxide and sodium metasilicate are favorites
for removing organic deposits, while acid or acid blends
are best for inorganic mineral deposits.

Traditionally, all of the brewery vessels were simply
scrubbed by hand and scalded with hot water; a few small
independent breweries still do it this way. Some fermentation methods (such as unions and stone squares) lend

themselves exclusively to this method because they employ wood or other porous material. Although such equipment can harbor bacteria, it would also be likely to harbor residues of any cleaning chemicals, which could be far worse for the beer and those who drink it.

For the homebrewer, hand scrubbing plus the use of a sanitizer like iodine or bleach should be adequate. Always visually inspect the surfaces of the vessels to make sure there are no obvious deposits before using them.

Brewing Throwback Mild

Brewing antique beers is a greater challenge. It requires a working knowledge of the history of brewing and long hours of research in old brewing texts, brewery logs, and trade journals. Fortunately, there are a number of good sources that tell us how the brewers of old made mild ales. The hard part is accurately substituting the raw materials that are available today for what those brewers would have been using 100, 200, or 300 years ago.

When interpreting old recipes, we must be sure to do it with the timeline of technological development in mind. For instance, when attempting to re-create a mild as it may have been brewed prior to 1817, it would be inaccurate to use any malts darker than brown malt. In those days, prior to the invention of the cylindrical drum roaster, attempts to kiln malt any darker would have turned the malt to charcoal. Unfortunately, brown malt as it was then is not available today. (See "Brown Malt" in chapter 3.)

The best we can do is assume that brown malts had some diastatic power in the early nineteenth century because they made up a large portion of some grist bills. (Modern brown malt has very little enzymatic power and is therefore useless as a base malt). We can use mild ale malt as the most authentic base malt available and substitute some middle-range crystal malts and perhaps some smoked malt for brown malts. Although this grist bill is probably very different from the original bills, we can feel reasonably comfortable with the accuracy of the substitution as it manifests itself in the final product.[1]

Hops are another problem. Who can be certain what the alpha acid content of hops was 100 or 200 years ago? Given that Goldings and Fuggle, introduced in 1850 and 1875 respectively, have replaced nearly every other hop variety (including such never-mentioned varieties as Farnham Pale and Long Square Garlic) in the United Kingdom, our best guess is to assume that Goldings and Fuggle were deemed better than the other varieties without compromising flavor and aroma.

Indeed, many of these varieties of hops were local favorites, probably harsh in flavor and cultivated because they were disease resistant or produced a higher yield per acre, rather than because of their character.[2] This practical reality, in combination with current practices among mild producers, leaves little doubt that Fuggle and Goldings are the way to go when brewing a throwback mild.

One other note on antique hops. Judging from the astronomical quantities of hops quoted in most contemporary sources of recipes from past centuries and the analysis of the wild hops from which they were bred, it is almost certain that the historical varieties were lower in alpha acids than most modern hops.

It is impossible to know what kind of yeast the brewers of old were using in their beers. Indeed, they themselves had no idea what they were using until Pasteur figured it out in 1876. The best we can do is use a modern yeast that seems to fit the prescription as far as attenuation goes. For instance, if a recipe calls for a relatively large quantity of hops, we can assume that the yeast was not very attenuative and the extra bitterness was needed to counter the sweetness left in the beer.

As far as brewing methods and equipment are concerned, the procedures were passed on verbally from generation to generation, and the equipment was primitive at best. A small, rather inefficient, homebrew set-up would best approximate the older systems, and the older procedures would have been devoid of even the simplest instrumentation. The recipes and calculations were based solely on the repeatability within the confines of that particular system.

For a very good original treatise on the art of brewing in the seventeenth century, read *A Guide to Gentlemen Farmers and Housekeepers for Brewing the Finest Malt Liquors* by Richard Bradley (available as a reprint; see "Further Reading" in the appendixes).

CHAPTER 5

Conditioning, Packaging, and Dispensing

Beer that has completed primary fermentation but contains very little carbonation and has not been allowed to mature is referred to as green beer. Most often, the maturation, or conditioning, process is carried out in closed containers that can handle some degree of pressure.

In theory, conditioning involves a secondary fermentation brought about by the small amount of yeast left in suspension, which metabolizes sugars that either escaped the primary fermentation or were added to the beer as priming sugar. In practice, however, cask fermentation is often a tertiary fermentation, following a short secondary fermentation that takes place at the brewery, although it is still common enough to find a brewery that racks directly into the trade casks.

One traditional method of conditioning is called *spünding* by German brewers. It involves either (1) choosing the exact time when there is enough fermentable sugar left in the beer to carbonate it with the carbon dioxide that is produced as a by-product or (2) closing the vessel so that the pressure builds and CO_2 dissolves into suspension.

The other, more common, English method of conditioning mild ale is to prime the fully fermented beer with a little sugar and perhaps a bit of new, lively yeast to do the job. The result is the same: the yeast metabolizes the sugar and the resulting CO_2 dissolves into suspension, carbonating the beer. In most mild ale breweries, these sugars are added as processed sugar (either cane, beet, or invert sugar). The carbon dioxide that is produced dissolves back into the beer in a closed cask and the beer comes into condition as a result.

In an alternative to this natural method of conditioning, extraneous carbon dioxide can be added directly to the beer and forced into solution. This is the method used by British keg beer producers, as well as by most American craftbrewers. However it is accomplished, the maturation process does more than condition the beer. The process causes other chemical changes to occur in the beer that produce changes in aroma and flavor, in addition to stabilizing and clarifying the final product.

The vast majority of mild ale produced in the United Kingdom is conditioned and served from a cask, but we can be reasonably certain that mild ales have, at some point in history, been bottle-conditioned. There are a number of examples of mild ales served cold and filtered from a pressurized keg (or a nitrogen keg) and filtered, force-carbonated, and bottled. In this section we will discuss these systems and their variations.

Cask Conditioning

> **Real ale**, a name for draught (or bottled) beer brewed from the traditional ingredients, matured by secondary fermentation in the container from which it is dispensed, and served without the use of extraneous carbon dioxide.
>
> —*Oxford English Dictionary* (Second Edition)

Some brewers and beer historians still maintain that mild ales are simply the draught version of brown ales. While I disagree wholeheartedly with this oversimplification, it is a fact that the overwhelming majority of mild ale leaves the brewery in a cask to be served on draught.

In cask-conditioning, the beer undergoing maturation is racked (decanted) into trade casks of varying sizes. There it is allowed to continue fermenting slowly, either by way of the residual yeast feeding on the remaining sugars or as a result of dosing the beer with yeast or sugar or some combination to the two. Often a dose of finings (a collagen-based substance designed to attract beer hazing compounds and make them fall out of suspension) and sometimes a shot of whole hops for additional aroma are added to the casks. Some cask-conditioned beers are filtered and then re-dosed with sugar and yeast before being racked into the casks, but I have found no instances of this occurring in mild ale breweries.

The casks are shipped to the publican's house where they are stillaged, vented, spiled, and tapped. They are allowed to clarify and, once they are bright, served to the guests. Unfortunately, this practice

Racking line at a typical British independent brewery. These casks are all kilderkins, but most cask lines can fill anything from a pin to a 36-gallon barrel.

completely died out in the United States with the advent of Prohibition, and only recently has it begun to make a small comeback there. Usually instituted as part of a brewpub's program, the cost of equipment and training, coupled with the relative uncertainty and instability of the product in comparison to the ease of handling pressurized, kegged beers makes this an impractical method for all but the smallest, most committed packaging brewers in the United States.

The Six Elements of Cask Ale

The Ale

Of course, the first element of cask ale to consider is the beer. Before determining variables like conditioning time or the volume of finings to be employed, we must first ascertain the condition the beer is already in. The amount of fermentable sugar still in solution, the degree to which the beer has already dropped bright, and the age of the beer at the time of racking will have a profound impact on the finished product in terms of flavor, clarity, and aroma.

For the most part, in making a mild ale, we are dealing with a malty, low-gravity beer that has a relatively low hop profile. In the case of throwback milds, the parameters do not change all that dramatically. With an increase in gravity, the ale will last longer after tapping (up to two weeks in the case of Sarah Hughes, says the brewer).

The beer should have undergone a good, active primary fermentation and have been allowed to age for not more than one week in secondary fermentation before racking. The beer should be a bit turbid (but not loaded with yeast silt), and the flavor and aroma profiles, suspended yeast and such notwithstanding, should be coming into line.

Hops

Although brewers are likely to use dry hops in the cask for their bitter ales, pale ales, and perhaps other products, they rarely use hops in casks of mild ale. At least three brewers I know of do use them—pointing to the hops' clarifying quality as the reason—but logic suggests, and other brewers confirm, that the benefit derived in terms of clarity can easily be had with finings.

In the opinion of most brewers, the benefit of using dry hops in the cask for mild ale does not outweigh the disadvantages of having an excess of hop aroma. If you do choose to use dry hops, pick a standard British variety like Goldings or Fuggle and then use it very sparingly. Bitter and pale ale brewers typically use 1-ounce plugs at the rate of 1 ounce to a firkin. I suggest using .5 ounce at most for mild ale.

The Cask

Filtered, carbonated beer comes in kegs. The correct term for the container that naturally conditioned beers come in is *cask*. Cask sizes are derived from an imperial barrel, which holds 2 gross (that is, 288) pints. Casks come in sizes that range from 4.5 U.K. gallons to 54 U.K. gallons. The most common casks sizes are firkins that hold 9 U.K. gallons or 10.8 U.S. gallons (see table 3).

Casks always have bowed sides and are fitted with a shive and keystone. The shive is fitted into a hole (known as the shive boss) in the very center of the cask's side, and the keystone is fitted into a hole in the head on the side furthest from the shive (known as the keystone boss). The keystone is fitted with a tap for dispensing; the shive is fitted with a spile, either hard or soft, for regulating the internal pressure and, thus, the level of carbonation in the beer.

At one time, all casks were wooden, and each brewery employed several coopers to build, maintain, and repair their casks. Today, with few exceptions, cooperage is

Mild Ale

TABLE 3

British Cask Names and Sizes

Cask Name	U.K. Gal.	U.S. Gal.	Liters
Pin	4.5 U.K. gal.	5.4 U.S. gal.	20.5 l
Firkin	9.0 U.K. gal.	10.8 U.S. gal.	41.0 l
Eleven	11.0 U.K. gal.[a]	13.2 U.S. gal.	50.0 l
Kilderkin	18.0 U.K. gal.	21.6 U.S. gal.	82.0 l
Twenty-two	22.0 U.K. gal.[a]	26.4 U.S. gal.	100.0 l
Barrel	36.0 U.K. gal.	43.2 U.S. gal.	123.0 l
Hogshead	54.0 U.K. gal.	64.8 U.S. gal.	141.0 l

Notes: A U.K. or imperial gallon is 1.2 U.S. gallons, so a firkin holds 10.8 U.S. gallons, and a kilderkin holds 21.6 gallons or 2 firkins. To further complicate matters, an imperial barrel-sized cask holds 43.2 U.S. gallons, but a U.S. barrel measure is only 31 U.S. gallons (24.8 U.K. gallons).

[a]These are metric sizes of 50 and 100 liters respectively. They are commonly called by their approximate imperial equivalent.

made of aluminum, stainless steel or, more rarely, enamel-lined mild steel. You must know which materials you are using in order to select the right cleaning agents. For example, strong alkalis like sodium hydroxide will corrode aluminum in a very short time, leaving it pock-marked and unsanitary.

Finings

Isinglass finings, which are used to help clarify the beer, are comprised of the dried, processed, swim bladders of selected fish (commonly the sturgeon). The bladders are processed by being soaked and dissolved in dilute solutions of cold tartaric and sulfurous acids. The result is a turbid, viscous solution made up chiefly of solubilized collagen. It works both as a function of electro-chemical attraction and mechanical floc-

Highgate casks lined up in the cellar of the White Horse on Parson's Green in London.

culation. The collagen is positively charged and therefore attracts negatively charged proteins, which increases the mass of both the finings and the proteins, causing them to fall out of suspension. Breweries may buy a prepared solution straight from a finings manufacturer or, in the case of several mild ale breweries such as Banks's, buy shredded bladders and manufacture the finings themselves.

There is an optimum rate for the addition of finings. Too little, and the beer will not be clarified; too much, and the sediment will be loose and fluffy—so much so that the mere action of drawing off beer through the tap will stir it. Unfortunately, there is no clear-cut proper dosage. It all depends upon the gravity of the beer, the suspended solids at the time of racking, and the conditions the beer will be faced with after racking.

The best advice I can offer is what has worked for me in the past. My colleagues and I have worked with several different brands of isinglass finings and have found that a sample mixed according to the directions of the manufacturer in the amount of 14 to 16 ounces per firkin gives the best results.

Often the mixing procedures are very complex, which put them outside the realm of feasibility for most pubs and microbrewers. However, these products will work for you, if you adhere to the recommended procedures as closely as possible. Sometimes this might mean simply mixing the finings in a blender on and off over the course of an hour or two before racking. One note of caution: I have found that finings of all sorts work best when fresh. Only mix enough to use in a single racking session.

Priming Sugar

To achieve the desired condition in a cask beer, it is often necessary to add a small amount of sugar to the cask prior to racking. This is especially true for low-gravity beers such as mild ale, where the primary fermentation is short and little residual sugar is left over.

Cask-conditioned beers typically contain 1.2 to 1.8 volumes of CO_2. That is, in one firkin of beer there will be 9 U.K. gallons of beer and between 10.8 and 16.2 U.K.

gallons of gaseous CO_2 at standard temperature and atmospheric pressure. (This might seem paradoxical, but dissolved CO_2 takes up only a small fraction of the space that gaseous CO_2 does.) To achieve the desired level of conditioning, the brewer must know the initial content of CO_2 in the green beer and then calculate the amount of sugar needed to produce the desired CO_2.

Green beer that has finished fermenting is naturally saturated with CO_2 as a result of the continuous stream of CO_2 bubbling through it during fermentation. The point

TABLE 4

Solubility of CO_2 at Atmospheric Pressure

Temperature (°C)	Volume CO_2	Temperature (°F)	Volume CO_2
0	1.70	32	1.70
2	1.60	35	1.60
4	1.50	40	1.45
6	1.40	45	1.30
8	1.30	50	1.20
10	1.20	55	1.10
12	1.12	60	1.00
14	1.05	65	0.92
16	0.99	70	0.85
18	0.93	75	0.78
20	0.88		
22	0.83		
24	0.78		
26	0.73		

of this saturation is entirely dependent on the temperature of the completed fermentation and the pressure in the tank. Table 4 lists the solubility of CO_2 in beer at atmospheric pressure. We will assume that the brewer is using the traditional method of open primary and secondary fermentation, and that fermentation at atmospheric pressure equals 14.7 pounds per square inch (psi).

Determining the amount of priming sugar to use in a cask is a function of the initial volumes of CO_2 and the fact that 4 grams of sucrose per liter of beer will yield approximately 1 volume of CO_2 (.5 ounce to 1 U.S. gallon → 1 volume CO_2).

For example, we will assume that a dark mild ale produced in a traditional Victorian tower brewery with open primary and secondary fermentation is racked from the secondary into casks at 18 °C (.93 volumes CO_2). The brewery specifications for this dark mild ale call for it reaching the publican with 1.6 volumes of CO_2 dissolved. We will use a 100% fermentable sucrose (pure cane, beet, or invert sugar) for priming.

An additional .67 volumes is needed to reach the desired condition. The calculation would follow this sequence: 4 grams sucrose × .67 volumes = 2.68 grams sucrose per liter = 110 grams per firkin, OR .5 ounce sucrose × .67 volumes = .335 ounce per U.S. gallon = 3.6 ounces per firkin.

Mild ale breweries use various kinds of sugar for priming, but chief among them are white cane or beet sugars; invert sugar runs a close second to the other two. These sugars are fully fermentable. Cane and invert sugars are used in both their crystalline and syrup forms. When using syrups, note that the fermentability per weight of sugar is reduced because of the substantial water content of syrup.

Dextrose, or corn sugar, is often preferred by home-brewers because many think that cidery flavors are supposedly imparted by cane sugar. I have never gotten cidery flavors using cane sugar, and as far as I know, there is no scientific support for this belief. The reported cidery flavors are more likely to stem from the use of inferior malt extracts, insufficient pitching rates, or using too much non-malt-derived sugar in the wort.

Sugars like common brown sugar can impart an interesting, caramelized flavor to the finished beer. Brown sugar does, though, contain some unfermentable sugar, and the weight should be adjusted accordingly—not more than an additional 15%.

Honey, maple syrup, molasses (treacle), and golden syrup can all be used as priming sugar, though the composition of these substances in terms of fermentability require that the weights used be substantially increased

(40% for honey, 50% for maple syrup, 80% for molasses, and 30% for golden syrup). For example, you would need to substitute 14 ounces of honey or 18 ounces of molasses for 10 ounces of sugar. (Again, be sure that the molasses contains no sulfites as a preservative.)

Yeast

Yeast is the final element the brewer needs to consider when producing cask beer. The brewer wants to be certain that the chosen yeast will condition the beer in a reasonable amount of time (without the brewer having to inoculate the beer with an excessive quantity), that it will fall out of suspension in a reasonable time and leave the beer bright, and that it will not impart an unpleasant aroma or flavor. In practice, it is best to use the same yeast strain you used to produce the beer—a small quantity will do the job. In terms of cell count, the beer should contain between .75 and 2 billion cells per milliliter when it is racked into the trade casks.

Racking

Assuming that you have adhered to sound brewing principals in the production of your mild ale, there does not have to be any change in the normal process for cask-conditioning through secondary fermentation.

To rack beer into a cask, fit a keystone into the keystone boss of a clean cask. Then add isinglass finings, priming sugar, yeast (if necessary), and dry hops (if you chose to use them). To prevent a protein haze, you may want to consider using an auxiliary fining like silica gel. Add 5–10 ounces of the auxiliary fining per firkin at the lowest temperature that the beer will encounter during its time in the cask.

Modern casking-lines pressurize the cask to just over atmospheric pressure, ensuring that the beer will not foam too much and decrease the quantity of beer that gets into the cask. A brewer can achieve the same results on a smaller scale simply by racking very slowly. Avoid picking up any yeast and proteins that may have settled to the bottom of the secondary fermenter. Only clean beer should make it into the cask.

As with any method of packaging, oxygen should be avoided. We are, however, better off than we would be if we were filtering and carbonating the beer because it is still alive, and any oxygen that might inadvertently make its way in will be used up in the aerobic life cycle of the yeast still in suspension.

When the cask is full, set and drive the shive home. Roll the cask thoroughly to ensure that the finings and priming sugar have mixed into the ale well. Then put the cask aside for storage. It is best to store the cask at or slightly below cellar temperature (50–56 °F, 10–13 °C), as the CO_2 will dissolve into the beer more readily at lower temperatures, and any possible microbial contaminants will be less likely to gain a foothold if kept cool.

Stillaging, Spiling, and Serving

The cask should be stored in an environment as close as possible to the actual cellar temperature until it is ready to be stillaged. The cask can be moved around, but not too much. There is evidence to suggest that the finings actually work best after the third or fourth mixing. When ready for stillaging, the cask must be supported on a slight angle toward the keystone, so it does not rock or shake. The goal is maximum stability, so that nothing will rouse the sediment at the bottom of the cask or cause any of the top break (the sediment floating at the top) to fall into the beer.

A very effective method of stillaging is to use either the wooden stillions sold for that purpose or to use three wedges (two at the front and one at the rear) to support the cask. Be sure that the bilge, the largest diameter portion of the cask directly in the center, does not touch the surface upon which the wedges are resting.

Once the cask has been stabilized, allow it to reach the ideal serving temperature—if the cask is too warm, not enough CO_2 will be dissolved into the solution, and if you were to then vent the cask, you might be dooming the beer to being under condition. At that point, the cask is ready to tap and spile.

The shive contains a center section called the tut, which can be punched through to allow CO_2 out and air in to avoid drawing a vacuum. The cask must be vented by piercing the tut with a soft spile. Many cellarmen pierce the tut with a specially made tool or with the small end of a valve-lifter from an old engine, but beware—the sudden loss of pressure when open-venting could stir the sediment at the bottom of the cask and result in a gushing of good beer all over the cellar floor. With a soft spile, the venting is more controlled because the spile is porous enough for CO_2 and a little beer foam to pass through. Once this liveliness has subsided, the soft spile can be replaced with a nonporous hard spile and the cask can be tapped and served.

The most traditional method of dispensing the beer is by letting gravity draw it out of the cask and into the glass. But because most cellars are found in the basements of pubs, it is more common today to find the cask stillaged in the cellar and the beer pumped up to the bar by means of a hand-pull beer engine or, in the case of at least one mild ale brewery, by an electric pump—though Campaign for Real Ale (CAMRA) purists decry the use of such devices. The beer then often runs through a sparkler (at the discretion of the brewer), which aerates the beer a little and knocks the CO_2 out of suspension to form a creamy head of very tiny, long-lasting bubbles. The alternative—serving without a sparkler—leaves more condition in the beer and less head in the glass.

Cellarmanship—the art of handling cask-conditioned real ale—is a very complex discipline that requires the understanding of hundreds of variables and the nuances of the particular beer you are handling. The preceding description is only meant to serve as a general guide. For a more detailed discussion of handling cask beers, read the CAMRA guide to *Cellarmanship*, available through CAMRA in the United Kingdom, or pick up a copy of *The Perfect Pint: Producing Real Ale in America*, by Ray Daniels (see "Appendix B: Further Reading").

Bottle Conditioning

The first bottled beers were undoubtedly bottled by hand, directly out of the trade casks, and sealed. These bottlings may have been relatively sound because the beer was still alive (there were a few living yeast cells to lend it some stability), but the beer would have ceased to be real ale by the modern definition. Another method of producing real ale—and the most common method in home-brewing circles—is by carrying out the secondary fermentation in bottles. Many of the same considerations apply to bottle-conditioned beer as to cask-conditioned beer, with the notable exception of finings. Rarely, if ever, do producers of bottle-conditioned beers use finings in the package. They have been known, however, to fine the beer with isinglass in a secondary fermentation vessel before bottling. Also, it is a common practice to run the beer through a coarse filtration and then prime it with a small amount of yeast and sugar to produce the conditioning that is desired.

The calculations used to determine priming sugar dosages applies here as well, whether or not you are filtering before bottling. Although it may be tempting to add the sugar directly to each bottle, it is advisable to add all the sugar and yeast (if necessary) at once to all the beer in a racking vessel. Fill and cap the bottles after the priming has been done. Conditioning should take place at a slightly warmer temperature (65–70 °F, 18–21 °C) for a week. After that, it should be returned to the ideal serving temperature (50–54 °F, 10–12 °C) for at least 14 to 21 days before serving.

A good, flocculent yeast strain will leave very compact "bottoms," or yeast sediment, at the bottom of the bottle. Be careful not to disturb this sediment when decanting the beer.

Force Conditioning

The most common method of conditioning in the world, and the method used at most pub and microbreweries, is force-carbonation. The beer should be as completely fermented as possible, and it should already have been fined or filtered. Chill the beer to as low a temperature as possible without freezing (33–38 °F, 5–3 °C, is sufficient) and then apply CO_2 from a cylinder at a pressure consistent with the volumes CO_2 chart in the appendixes. Shake the keg every few minutes until the flow of CO_2 into the container stops.

If conditioning a large volume of beer, it is best to use a perforated carbonation/aeration stone to do the job. The stone has very tiny pores that let the CO_2 through in small streams, increasing the gas-to-beer contact ratio and therefore decreasing the time required to fully carbonate.

No matter how you condition the beer, mild ale should be drunk from a proper English pint glass or pewter tankard; that is, one containing a full 20 ounces of ale. Inasmuch as mild ale is of relatively low alcohol content but offers profound flavor, this method of serving should appeal to modern sensibilities, which dictate moderation in the consumption of intoxicating beverages while encouraging indulgence in richness and quality of flavor.

CHAPTER 6

Commercially Produced Mild Ales

The *CAMRA Real Mild Guide* for 1998 lists 137 mild ales being produced in the United Kingdom (see appendix A). This may sound like quite a few milds, but the overall barrelage being produced as compared to bitter and even old ale is very low. Some of the breweries listed in the guide, such as Adnam's of Suffolk and Hanson's, are no longer producing the mild or have sold the brand names to other breweries. Adnam's is selling the brand name to a Black Country brewer, and Hanson's Mild, which has been brewed by Wolverhampton and Dudley breweries (of Banks's fame) is being phased out in favor of the Banks's label.

Hanson's Mild, brewed by Wolver-hampton and Dudley breweries, is being phased out in favor of its more famous sister, Banks's.

What follows is a listing of some of the better-known, more commonly available milds as well as a few American examples. The analytical data presented here are for 10 mild ales ranging from light to dark and from low gravity to rather bawdy. I believe it represents a fair cross-section of what constitutes mild ale as it exists today. Table 5 shows the composition of several mild ales in terms of malts, adjuncts, and the types of hops used in them, providing some indication, in percentages, of where the fermentable sugars come from in some typical mild ales.

Unfortunately, the truest milds—those brewed in their native England—are not available in the United States. Therefore, those who wish to try them are completely out of luck unless they are willing to travel or are able to cajole a friend into bringing them back one of the few bottled examples, such as Sarah Hughes or Cain's Dark Mild.

If you are in the United Kingdom and are searching for a bottled mild, beware. Most brewers who bottle their

TABLE 5

An Analysis of Several Mild Ale Formulations

	W-H 1[a]	W-H 2[a]	Bateman's DM	Highgate Dark Mild	Holden's Mild	McMullen's AK	Sarah Hughes Ruby Red
OG (°P)	11.2	10.0	8.3	8.9	9.2	8.3	14.2
SG	1.045	1.04	1.033	1.0355	1.037	1.033	1.058
FG (°P)	NA	NA	1.3	2.3	2.1	1.5	3.6
FG (SG)	NA	NA	1.005	1.009	1.008	1.006	1.014
Pale	76.9%	66.5%	60.0%	70.0%	90.0%	79.0%	75.0%
Brown/amber	2.8%	6.5%	—	—	—	—	—
Crystal	2.8%	—	12.0%	10.0%	—	—	25.0%
Chocolate	—	—	5.0%[b]	—	—	1.0%	—
Roasted barley	—	—	—	—	5.0%	—	—
Black	—	—	—	2.0%	—	—	—
Torrified barley	—	—	—	6.0%	—	—	—
Wheat malt	—	7.1%	—	—	—	—	—
Torrified wheat	—	—	4.0%	—	—	—	—
Flaked maize	—	—	—	—	—	6.0%	—
Sugar	17.5%	19.9%	19.0%	12.0%	5.0%	14.0%	—
IBU	NA	NA	22	22	24	22	30
Kettle hops	NA	NA	Golding	Golding	Fuggle and Golding	Golding	Fuggle and Golding
Late hops	NA	NA	Golding	Golding	Golding	None	Golding

Notes: NA = Not listed in the source.

[a]Data from Wahl-Henius, *The American Handy-Book of Brewing and Auxiliary Trades* (Chicago: Wahl-Henius Institute, 1908).

[b]The commercial version of this recipe uses brewers' caramel for color; the chocolate malt shown here approximates the color of the commercial product.

mild ale do so under the name "brown ale" for reasons that I cannot figure out—and they have been unable to explain, though the practice probably has its roots in the mad rush to capitalize on the success of bottled Newcastle Brown Ale in the 1920s and 1930s. Holden's, Everard's, Boddington's, Bateman's, and Kimberley and Morrell's of Oxford all make exceptional mild ales but bottle their products as brown ale, while some like Sarah Hughes, Brains, and Ansells bottle under the name mild ale.

Highgate—the Champion Mild of Britain, 1997.

Luckily, however, if you are unable to try the British milds, there are many fine examples being brewed in the United States, and the number is growing daily. I have found exceptional milds at Commonwealth Brewery in Boston, Massachusetts; Goose Island Beer Company in Chicago, Illinois; and at Deschutes Brewery in Bend, Oregon. For a real treat, try Marblehead Mild–the gold medal winner in the English-Style Brown Ale category at the 1998 Great American Beer Fesitval. It is brewed by Salem Beer Works in Salem, Massachusetts.

Highgate Dark Mild

Brewers: Highgate and Walsall Brewing Company, Ltd., Sandymount Road, Walsall, West Midlands WS1 3AP, United Kingdom. Telephone: (01922) 644453.

Brewing Specifics

OG:	1.035 (8.9 °P)
TG:	1.009 (2.3 °P)
ABV:	3.1%
IBUs:	22
Hop variety:	Golding throughout
Malt:	Pale, crystal, black, and chocolate
Adjuncts:	Brewers' caramel in the boil, and cane sugar to prime
Mash:	Single-temperature infusion at 155 °F (68 °C)
Boil:	90 minutes
Fermentation:	Open wooden squares, some lined with UHMW plastic
Yeast:	House culture that consists of a mix of four separate strains
Packaging:	100% cask-conditioned

Entering an area of small, neighborhood shops and multifamily houses in the largely residential village of Walsall, one must negotiate a maze of winding side streets to find the venerable Victorian building which, for the last 100 years, has housed the Highgate Brewery. Built in 1898 to generic, "off-the-shelf" plans, Highgate's six-story brick facility exemplifies a standard Victorian tower brewery. In fact, the well-preserved building now is listed on Britain's national historic register.

The brewery takes its name from the old "high gate" that once stood in front of the brewery and allowed access to old Walsall. And while Highgate produces a very good best bitter (Saddler's Best Bitter, 1.045 SG, 3.2% ABV, with an absolutely breathtaking Styrian Golding character) and an Old Ale (a higher-gravity version of the mild, with much more fruitiness), its principal product always has been its dark mild.

The brewery still works in classic tower fashion, with only three pumps to do all the work. The 70-barrel brewery, which operates much as it did in 1898, features an original wooden malt-screening device affectionately called the coffin, thanks to its similar shape; two original wooden mash tuns, now clad and lined with stainless steel; and twin original copper brew kettles. Fermentation occurs in open oak squares now lined with white UHMW plastic. The basement of the brewery houses the racking department and yeast storage.

Until a management buyout in 1995, Highgate had been the smallest brewery in the Bass conglomerate for a decade. Its flagship dark mild was changed by the Bass marketing department to Highgate Dark. Neil Bain, the current CEO and brewmaster, changed the name back. He says that he and his staff are proud to call their mild by its real name.

Highgate Dark Mild is a mahogany-colored brew with a tight off-white head, when served properly. Its aroma is fruity, with notes of apples, caramel, and vanilla. Vanilla, Highgate's signature characteristic, also shows up in the beer's flavor, along with dark fruit, caramel, a bit of nutty malt, and just a hint of bitterness in the dry finish. Highgate is brewed to 1.055 SG and watered down to 1.035 SG before fermentation. The mild has received numerous awards, including CAMRA's "Midlands Mild of the Year" award.

It is interesting to note that Highgate shares its own house strain with other area mild ale brewers. Highgate retains the services of the laboratories at Bass in Burton-on-Trent to keep the strain pure and to repropagate it every 16 generations.

Walnut Mild

Brewers: Marston, Thompson, and Evershed PLC, Shobnall Road, Burton-on-Trent, Staffordshire DE14 2BW, United Kingdom. Telephone: (01283) 531131.

Brewing Specifics

OG:	1.035 (8.75 °P)
TG:	1.009 (2.2 °P)
ABV:	3.5%

Brewing Specifics (*continued*)

IBUS:	NA
Hop variety:	East Kent Golding throughout
Malt:	Pipkin pale, crystal, and chocolate
Adjuncts:	Invert sugar in copper and priming
Mash:	Single-temperature at 52 °R^a (150 °F, 65.5 °C)
Boil:	1 hour
Fermentation:	Entirely in Burton Unions
Yeast:	Very powdery union yeast that is unique to Marston's
Packaging:	Cask-conditioned and bottle-conditioned

^{a}°R = Degrees Reaumur, a temperature scale used solely in the brewing industry, which Marston's uses.

Marston's has become a sort of Mecca for beer aficionados. It is the last user of the very costly, once-famous Burton Union system of fermentation. Famous for the pale ales of its past and for the Pedigree bitter of its present, Marston's history is firmly rooted in mild ale—firmly enough that the word "MILD" is forever emblazoned alongside of "PALE" and "OLD" on one of the three barrels in the company's logo.

One of the rotating selections in the Brewer's Choice line of beer, Walnut Mild represents the lowest-gravity beer in Marston's product line. Like its cousin, the throwback mild called Merrie Monk, Walnut is entirely fermented in the unions, unlike Marston's other beers, which contain only a small percentage of union-fermented beer (the bulk of those other beers is fermented in large open squares). Walnut Mild is a classic dark mild, reminiscent of Highgate Dark Mild. Huge chocolate flavor and a maltiness untouched by hops make this an extremely enjoyable session beer. You get the feeling you are drinking a much bigger beer as it goes down your throat.

Banks's

Brewers: Wolverhampton and Dudley Breweries PLC, P.O. Box 26, Park Brewery, Bath Road, Wolverhampton, West Midlands WV1 4NY, United Kingdom. Telephone: (01902) 711811.

Brewing Specifics

OG:	1.036 (9 °P)
TG:	NA
ABV:	3.5%
IBUs:	18
Hop variety:	Fuggle
Malt:	Pale and crystal
Adjuncts:	Sugar, presumably sucrose, in the copper; brewers' caramel for coloring
Mash:	Single-temperature infusion, 152 °F (66.5 °C)
Boil:	60 minutes
Fermentation:	Open squares
Yeast:	House strain
Packaging:	Cask, bottle, and keg

Banks's is the flagship product of Wolverhampton and Dudley Breweries, the largest regional brewery in the Black Country. Although Banks's is known widely as a mild ale, the brewery has recently opted to drop the "mild" moniker in favor of the simple brand name, in an attempt to lose the cloth-cap image and rejuvenate the brand.

Critics of Banks's claim that the beer is simply a colored-up version of Wolverhampton and Dudley's bitter, which is gaining rapidly on the mild in terms of total

barrels produced. However, a taste of the beer leaves little doubt that this is not entirely true. It is a nice amber color, which the brewery admits is the product of coloring after fermentation, but it is definitely maltier than their bitter, which smacks heavily of Goldings. Perhaps the difference is wholly in the dry-hopping, but the background caramel flavor in the mild suggests that a larger percentage of the grist for the mild is crystal as compared to the grist for the bitter.

Holden's Black Country Mild

Brewers: Timonthy Holden, Holden's Brewery Co. Ltd., Holden Brewery, George Street, Woodsetton, Dudley, West Midlands DY1 4LN, United Kingdom. Telephone: (01902) 80051.

Brewing Specifics

OG:	1.037 (9.2 °P)
TG:	1.008 (2.1 °P)
ABV:	3.7%
IBUS:	NA (likely in the low 20s)
Hop variety:	Golding and Brambling Cross
Malt:	Pale, crystal, and roasted barley
Adjuncts:	Sucrose in copper and at priming
Mash:	Single-temperature infusion
Boil:	90 minutes
Fermentation:	Open
Yeast:	House strain, a true top-cropper
Packaging:	Casks and bottles; a few kegs as well

Although one of the better known mild ale brewers, Holden's chooses to call their bottled mild a brown ale.

One of the long-established family breweries of the Black Country, Holden's started as a brewpub at the Park

Inn (now Holden's brewery tap) in 1916. It produces a good range of ales for more than 20 tied houses and more than 100 free-trade customers.

Although darker than many milds, Holden's Black Country Mild is very light in flavor. A worthy nod to the malt, the hop presence is just barely perceptible. Roasted barley is used for the color, but it is not readily apparent in the flavor profile. This ale drinks with the body of a much stronger beer.

Dark Ruby Mild

Brewers: Guy Perry, Sarah Hughes Brewery, Beacon Hotel, 129 Bilston Street, Sedgley, Dudley, West Midlands DY3 1JE, United Kingdom. Telephone: (01902) 883380.

Brewing Specifics

OG:	1.058 (14.5 °P)
TG:	NA
ABV:	6.0%
IBUs:	32
Hop variety:	Variable, usually Goldings
Malt:	Paul's pale, crystal, chocolate, and roasted barley
Adjuncts:	Invert sugar in the copper and for priming
Mash:	Single-temperature infusion
Boil:	90 minutes in open-top copper
Fermentation:	Open fermentation in converted Grundy tanks
Yeast:	Borrowed from Holden's or Highgate
Packaging:	Cask- and bottle-conditioned; sold mainly on premise

Sarah Hughes is a brewpub and microbrewery in the richly appointed Victorian-style conservatory of the Beacon Hotel in Sedgley, United Kingdom. The brewery is about 125 years old, but it laid dormant for 20 years after the current owner's grandmother, Sarah Hughes, died. In 1987, John Hughes revived the brewery to service the hotel and a few other outlets.

The classic throwback mild, Original Ruby Mild, harkens back to the earlier days of mild ale, boasting a whopping 6% ABV. (The brewery's pale ale, Sedgley Surprise, is only 1.048 OG, 5% ABV.) Original Ruby has a full, sweet, and malty palate and unleashes a blitz of clean, fruity flavors. The ale's body is huge, edging on syrupy.

McMullen's AK

Brewers: McMullen and Sons Ltd., Hertford Brewery, 26 Old Cross, Hertford SG14 1RD, England. Telephone: (01992) 500729.

Brewing Specifics

OG:	1.033 (8.25 °P)
TG:	1.006 (1.7 °P)
ABV:	3.6%
IBUS:	22
Hop variety:	Goldings for bitterness and aroma, plus dry-hopping in the cask

Brewing Specifics (*continued*)

Malt:	79% pale, 1% chocolate
Adjuncts:	6% flaked maize in the mash, 14% glucose and invert sugar in copper, and cane sugar for priming
Mash:	Single-temperature infusion at 148 °F (64.5 °C)
Boil:	90 minutes
Fermentation:	Open fermentation at 68–70 °F (20–21 °C)
Yeast:	Top-cropping house strain
Packaging:	Cask-conditioned

McMullen and Sons was founded in Hertford, Hertfordshire, in 1827 and began producing its flagship product, known simply as AK, in 1832. The designation "AK" was not unique to McMullen's—there were at least a dozen other brews using that moniker at the time—but McMullen's is the only example that survived. Beer historian Martyn Cornell theorizes that it stands for *ale kyte*, Flemish for "small beer." Whatever the origin of the name, McMullen's AK is the most widely known example of light or pale mild in the world.

McMullen's Brewery in Hertford exemplifies the ornate architecture of Victorian tower breweries.

Although the name "pale mild" was dropped

in the early 1990s, AK is made with pale and chocolate malts to 1.034 SG and 3.7% ABV. McMullen's AK starts with a dry maltiness and rounds out with a nice tea-like finish imparted by Goldings hops.[1]

In addition to their famous AK, McMullen's has also brewed a dark mild bottled as a brown ale.

Bateman's DM

Brewers: George Bateman and Son Ltd., Salem Bridge Brewery, Mill Lane, Wainfleet, Skegness, Lincolnshire PE24 4JE, England. Telephone: (01754) 880317.

Brewing Specifics

OG:	1.033 (8.25 °P)
TG:	1.005 (1.2 °P)
ABV:	3.0%
IBUs:	22
Hop variety:	Goldings for bitterness and aroma as well as dry hopping in the cask.
Malt:	Pale, crystal, and brewers' caramel for color
Adjuncts:	Caramel in the boil, and cane sugar for priming
Mash:	Single-temperature infusion
Boil:	90 minutes
Fermentation:	Open fermentation at 68–70 °F (20–21 °C)
Yeast:	Top-cropping house strain
Packaging:	Cask-conditioned

Bateman's bottles its DM *as a nut brown ale.*

Founded in 1874, Bateman's is the last remaining brewery in the whole of Lincolnshire (an English county best known for the Norman cathedral and castle of its capital city). The brewery has prospered over the past several years, finding new markets for its beers, both at home and abroad—including America, where craft-beer consumers have embraced Bateman's complex XXXB ale (5% ABV) and potent Victory Ale (6% ABV).

Visitors to Wainfleet can locate Bateman's by looking for its crenellated tower, which rises above the area's thatched cottages and rambling fields. Originally built as a windmill serving a local bakery, this tower (now missing its sails) was annexed by the adjacent brewery in the 1920s. It presently houses the all-important sample room. The administrative offices and whitewashed brew house still occupy their century-old sites next door.

Bateman's DM hails from the coast of the North Sea north of East Anglia—well outside the mild ale stronghold of the West Midlands. Nevertheless, it took the title "Champion Mild of Britain" at the Great British Beer Festival in 1997. It is dark, molasses-brown in color and the aroma is not unlike molasses or dark brown sugar. The beer delivers a full, toasty palate. Malt is clearly the signature flavor here, but a pleasant bitterness takes the edge off the sweetness.

Gateway Dark

Brewers: Brian O'Reilly, David Sutula, and Bill Bryson, John Harvard's Brew House #13, 1087 Old River Road, Cleveland, Ohio 44113. Telephone: (216) 623-2739.

Brewing Specifics

OG:	1.033 (8.3 °P)
TG:	1.005 (1.2 °P)
ABV:	3.1%
IBUs:	21
Hop variety:	Willamette
Malt:	Pale, crystal, chocolate
Adjuncts:	Flaked maize in the mash, and cane sugar to prime
Mash:	Single-temperature infusion at 152 °F (66.5 °C)
Boil:	2 hours total (90 minutes with hops)
Fermentation:	Closed, dual-stage fermentation
Yeast:	Whitbread, top-cropping strain
Packaging:	Served cask-conditioned or filtered

The John Harvard's Brew House chain of brewpubs was founded in Cambridge, Massachusetts, in 1992. Since then, the company has grown to over 14 stores in the eastern United States. Brewpub number 13 was opened in Cleveland, Ohio, in September of 1997 under the "Honest Food, Real Beer" banner that each of the chain's brewpubs flies.

Formerly called Gateway Mild, Gateway Dark was originally filtered and nitrogenated. In addition to changing the name, the brewery began to serve the beer filtered and carbonated, occasionally offering it gravity-dispensed from a firkin or served through a hand pump.

Gateway Dark is a deep brown color, with ruby highlights. The aroma is reminiscent both of chocolate malt and fresh tobacco from the Willamette hops used for bittering and aroma. The body is light and dry, while chocolate malt predominates over toffee and molasses notes. The cask-conditioned versions have in the past been done without dry hops, with Willamette dry hops, or with Styrian Goldings. I personally favor the character of the Willamettes over the Styrians in this particular beer.

Harvard's AK

Brewers: Brian O'Reilly, David Sutula, and Bill Bryson at John Harvard's Brew House #13, 1087 Old River Road, Cleveland, Ohio 44113. Telephone: (216) 623-2739.

Brewing Specifics

OG:	1.033 (8.2 °P)
TG:	1.007 (1.75 °P)
ABV:	3.1%
IBUS:	19
Hop variety:	Willamette, Styrian Goldings
Malt:	Pale and crystal
Adjuncts:	Flaked corn in the mash
Mash:	Single-temperature infusion at 152 °F (66.5 °C)
Boil:	2 hours total (90 minutes with hops)
Fermentation:	4 days at 68 °F (20 °C), transferred to secondary at 50 °F (10 °C), and cooled to 33 °F (.5 °C) before filtration
Yeast:	Top-cropping strain of London origin
Packaging:	Served cask-conditioned or cold with forced carbonation

This is another offering from John Harvard's Brew House number 13 that is modeled after the famous pale mild, Original AK, from McMullen's in Hertford. Harvard's AK is a bit drier and less sweet than the original, with a bit less hop presence than the British version. The people of Cleveland have come to enjoy this crisp and refreshing brew during hot summer nights on the patio in the Cleveland flats.

PMD **Mild**

Brewers: Gregory Hall, Goose Island Beer Company, 1800 N. Clybourn Ave., Chicago, Illinois 60614. Telephone: (312) 915-0071.

Brewing Specifics

OG:	1.034 (8.5 °P)
TG:	1.010 (2.5 °P)
ABV:	2.5 %
IBUs:	22
Hop variety:	Fuggles throughout
Malt:	American two-row, caramel (40 °L), and wheat malt
Adjuncts:	None
Mash:	Single-temperature infusion
Boil:	100 minutes, 90 minutes with hops
Fermentation:	3 days primary fermentation at 68 °F (20 °C), 3-day diacetyl rest at 70 °F (21 °C)
Yeast:	Top-cropping house strain
Packaging:	Served cask-conditioned or cold with forced carbonation

Among the fastest growing craftbrewers in the nation, Goose Island Beer Company was founded in 1988 by owner John Hall in Chicago's burgeoning Clybourn Corridor, once the center of the city's pre-Prohibition brewing district. With a 2,500-barrel annual output, the Clybourn brewpub has been recognized as one of the top ten breweries in the world by the prestigious Beverage Testing Institute.

The success of this original brewpub prompted the 1995 launch of Goose Island's second facility, a 37,000-square-foot, state-of-the-art brewery on West Fulton Street. It includes a high-speed bottling line that will enable the company to produce over 100,000 barrels annually. This expanded capacity will also aid in the distribution of Goose Island's award-winning Honker's Ale and its seasonal beers, which are sent to over 1,000 locations.

PMD Mild has the distinction of being one of only two mild ales to have won a medal at the Great American Beer Festival to date: the gold medal in the English-Style Brown Ale category for 1995. It is also the only mild ale listed on Michael Jackson's *Beer Hunter* CD-ROM as a world classic beer. (It is interesting that a British beer writer would award this honor to an American example of a beer style that is so uniquely English.)

PMD takes its name from the Protected Manufacturing District, which is where the original Goose Island brew-pub sits. The district is reminiscent of the industrial sprawl of the English Midlands. This beer, with its delicate malt nose and caramel flavors, is a fitting tribute to the people of Chicago and the Midlands who owe their livelihood to industry.

PMD is a dark mild with a great Fuggle character in the palate and subtle bitterness that does nothing to impair the delicate sweetness of the malt. This mild is devoid of any diacetyl, and yeast character is minimal, if present at all. A delicious example—the best I've found outside the Midlands, and perhaps better than many of them.

Commonwealth Best Mild

Brewers: Jeffrey Charnick, Commonwealth Brewing Company Ltd., 138 Portland Street, Boston, Massachusetts 02114. Telephone: (617) 523-8383.

Brewing Specifics

OG:	1.046 (11.5 °P)
TG:	1.011 (2.8 °P)
ABV:	4.5%
IBUs:	28
Hop variety:	East Kent Goldings
Malt:	British pale, crystal, and chocolate
Adjuncts:	None
Mash:	Single-temperature infusion at 152 °F (66.5 °C)
Boil:	75 minutes with hops, 85 minutes total
Fermentation:	Open squares at 62–68 °F (16.5–20 °C)
Yeast:	True top-cropping house strain
Packaging:	Served cask-conditioned or cold with forced carbonation

Commonwealth Brewing Company, located in Boston, Massachusetts, is one of the staple East Coast brewpubs. One of the United States' largest producers and retailers of naturally conditioned beers, Commonwealth offers a wide variety of both British and Continental styles. It is a very traditional British-style brewery, employing everything from a hop back to a Steele's masher. This is a must-see brewery for connoisseurs of British ale.

Commonwealth Best Mild (CBM), a tawny example of a mild ale, is something of a throwback to the 1930s and 1940s mild in that no adjuncts are used in the mash or boil, and it has an atypically high original gravity and alcohol content. It's a very tasty beer with a big, bold body and crisp maltiness, with only the faintest hint of chocolate.

CHAPTER 7

Mild Ale
Recipes

This section presents seven formulations that are representative of different types of commercially available milds. For each example, three different recipes will be given. The first is a 5-gallon (18.9-liter) all-grain recipe. Because most milds contain some adjunct sugar in the form of nonbarley cereal grains or the direct addition of sugar, the term *all-grain* will refer to beers made without any malt extract.

The second is a similar 5-gallon recipe using malt extract as the main source of fermentable sugar. The third is a stepped-up version of the first, aiming for a yield of 1 barrel (1.17 hectoliters). Craftbrewers who are using a multiple-barrel system in a pub or microbrewery can increase this single-barrel recipe by multiplying the values presented times the number of barrels to be produced.

Each of these recipes was brewed over the course of a month, using the ambient temperature of my basement (68 °F, 20 °C) as the primary fermentation temperature, secondary fermentation temperature, and conditioning temperature. All were brewed using a single-temperature infusion, and by converting for 50 minutes before starting to recirculate. Each was lautered in the same Phil's Lauter, which achieves a relatively consistent 81% efficiency. All were open-fermented with the same strain of yeast (Wyeast 1318 London Ale III, which I find to be an absolutely excellent strain for top-cropping) in a 10-gallon stainless-steel pot. Part of each recipe was bottle-conditioned, and the rest was kegged with force-carbonation.

Two of the ales, Abili Red Mild and Lusty Gnome Midlands Mild, were also cask-conditioned in a 4.5 U.K. gallon pin and served draught. Only one of these was actually brewed using the extract recipe listed (Mild Ale, c. 1824).

You will notice that all of the extract recipes call for steeping some of the malt. I believe that steeping grains adds a depth of character that is rarely achieved with all-extract recipes and, even if there were only a marginal improvement, it would still be worth the minimal effort steeping requires.

To gain the most from your steeping grains, first have the homebrew supplier you deal with crush the grains—or do it yourself with a corona mill or any of the wide variety of mills available to the small-scale brewer. Then put the grains in an oversized (loose) steeping bag; homebrew shops carry just the right thing, or you can make your own with cheese cloth or muslin. Immerse the bagged grains in the cold water you are going to brew with.

When brewing the all-grain recipes, be sure that your malt is well crushed. Remember that it is better to be under-crushed and lose the 60-cents-worth of extract than to have a stuck mash. And, speaking of mashing, remember to mash thick and stir well, checking to see that the temperature is even throughout the mash.

Sparge with water only a few degrees above the mash temperature, and boil rapidly for 60 to 90 minutes. After the boil, follow your normal procedures for separating the wort and trub (whirlpool, hop back, centrifuge) and cooling. The wort should be pitched with plenty of a good, healthy British yeast culture to $8 - 16 \times 10^6$ cells/ml. Watch the fermentation temperature so that it stays below 70 °F (21 °C).

When brewing with specialty grains, make sure the grains are well-crushed and place them inside a highly porous, net-like bag. Put the requisite volume of cold liquor (cold water) in the kettle (your pot has now become a kettle) and place the grains in it. Apply heat to the kettle, making sure that the grains are nice and wet inside the bag. Let the temperature rise to 160 °F (71 °C), and hold it there for 10 to 20 minutes.

Remove the grains, being certain to squeeze the last of the wort out before discarding them, and then add the malt extract. Proceed as usual with the rest of the brew, adding malt extract and sugar as required.

Notice that I only specify pale (unhopped) malt extract. I believe that the character derived from adding pellets (or whole hops) to the kettle is far superior to the character of hopped malt extracts and that the effect is well worth the minimal investment required.

Above all else, "Fret, sweat, and have a mild ale!"

AK

Malt	%	Grain, 5 Gal.	Extract, 5 Gal.	Grain, 1 Bbl.
Pale malt	80.0	5.00 lbs. (2.40 kg)	—	31.00 lbs. (14.1 kg)
Pale malt extract	80.0	—	4.50 lbs. (2.1 kg)	—
Chocolate malt	1.0	1.25 oz. (35.0 g)	1.25 oz. (35.0 g)	7.75 oz. (220.0 g)
Flaked maize	5.0	0.50 lb. (228.0 g)	0.50 lb. (228.0 g)	3.10 lbs. (1.4 kg)
Invert or cane sugar	14.0	17.50 oz. (500.0 g)	17.50 oz. (500.0 g)	6.80 lbs. (3.1 kg)

Bittering Hops (90 min.)	Grain, 5 Gal.	Extract, 5 Gal.	Grain, 1 Bbl.
Golding (5% alpha)	1.00 oz. (28.5 g)	1.00 oz. (28.5 g)	6.20 oz. (1.8 kg)
HBU	5	5	31
IBU	22	22	22

Brewing Specifics

Color:	6 °L
Mash temperature:	147 °F (64 °C)
OG:	1.033 (8.3 °P)
FG:	1.006 (1.5 °P)
Priming sugar:	2.00 oz. (57.0 g) cane sugar in 5 gal.
CO_2:	1.3–2.5 volumes
Packaging:	Draught or keg
Finings:	3.00 oz. isinglass to 5 gal.

Maclay's 56/Mild Ale (c. 1909)

Malt	%	Grain, 5 Gal.	Extract, 5 Gal.	Grain, 1 Bbl.
Pale ale malt	67.0	8.75 lbs. (4.0 kg)	—	55.00 lbs. (25.0 kg)
Light malt extract	67.0	—	7.50 lbs. (5.5 kg)	—
Black malt	1.8	3.75 oz. (107.0 g)	3.75 oz. (107.0 g)	1.50 lbs. (684.0 g)
Amber malt[a]	7.7	1.00 lb. (456.0 g)	1.00 lb. (456.0 g)	6.20 lbs. (2.8 kg)
Wheat malt	23.5	3.00 lbs. (1.4 kg)	3.00 lbs. (1.4 kg)	18.60 lbs. (10.5 kg)

Bittering Hops (90 min.)	Grain, 5 Gal.	Extract, 5 Gal.	Grain, 1 Bbl.
Golding (4% alpha)	4.00 oz. (114.0 g)	4.00 oz. (114.0 g)	1.50 lbs.
HBU	16	16	96
IBU	67	67	67

Brewing Specifics

Color:	11 °L
Mash temperature:	152 °F (66.5 °C)
OG:	1.060 (14.7 °P)
FG:	1.015 (3.8 °P)
Priming sugar:	2.00 oz. (57.0 g) cane sugar in 5 gal.
CO_2:	1.5–2.0 volumes
Packaging:	Draught or bottle-conditioned
Finings:	3.00 oz. isinglass to 5 gal. (if bottled, fine in a separate vessel, then rack the beer into a bottling bucket, prime, and bottle)

[a]Beeston Amber Malt.

Source: Converted from ledgers held at the Scottish Brewing Archive, Heriot-Watt University, Edinburgh, Scotland.

Abili Red Mild

Malt	Grain, 5 Gal.	Extract, 5 Gal.	Grain, 1 Bbl.
Pale malt	4.60 lbs. (2.1 kg)	—	28.50 lbs. (13.0 kg)
Pale malt extract	—	3.33 lbs. (1.5 kg)	—
Crystal malt	15.00 oz. (4.3 kg)	15.00 oz. (427.0 g)	5.80 lbs. (2.70 kg)
Chocolate malt	6.00 oz. (170.0 g)	6.00 oz. (170.0 g)	2.30 lbs. (1.05 kg)
Torrified wheat	5.00 oz. (142.0 g)	5.00 oz. (142.0 g)	1.90 lbs. (866.0 g)
Invert sugar (in kettle)	1.50 lbs. (684.0 g)	1.50 lbs. (684.0 g)	9.30 lbs. (4.24 kg)

Bittering Hops (90 min.)	Grain, 5 Gal.	Extract, 5 Gal.	Grain, 1 Bbl.
Golding (5% alpha)	1.00 oz. (57.0 g)	1.00 oz. (57.0 g)	6.25 oz. (353.0 g)
HBU	5.00	5.00	31.25
IBU	22	22	22

Aroma Hops (15 min.)	Grain, 5 Gal.	Extract, 5 Gal.	Grain, 1 Bbl.
Golding	0.33 oz. (10.0 g)	0.33 oz. (10.0 g)	2.00 oz. (57.0 g)

Brewing Specifics	
Color:	13 °L
Mash temperature:	149 °F (65 °C)
OG:	1.033 (8.3 °P)
FG:	1.005 (1.3 °P)
Priming sugar:	2.00 oz. (57.0 g) cane sugar in 5 gal.
CO$_2$:	1.5–2.5 volumes (if kegged)
Packaging:	Draught or keg
Finings:	3.00 oz. isinglass to 5 gal.

Note: Abili Red Mild is a pleasing, deep ruby red color and has a pleasing malty chewiness. Care should be taken to get this ale to attenuate very well. The caramel and roasted notes lend themselves well to a nice, dry finish.

KMS *Dark Mild*

Malt	%	Grain, 5 Gal.	Extract, 5 Gal.	Grain, 1 Bbl.
Pale malt	62	5.50 lbs. (2.5 kg)	—	34.10 lbs. (15.5 kg)
Pale malt extract	62	—	4.25 lbs. (1.9 kg)	—
Crystal malt	15	1.33 lbs. (600g)	1.33 lbs. (600.0 g)	8.25 lbs. (3.7 kg)
Chocolate malt	5	6.50 oz. (185g)	6.50 oz. (185.0 g)	2.50 lbs. (1.1 kg)
Flaked maize	8	10.50 oz. (300g)	10.50 oz. (300.0 g)	4.00 lbs. (1.8 kg)
Invert or cane Sugar	10	13.50 oz. (385g)	13.50 oz. (385.0 g)	5.25 lbs. (2.4 kg)

Bittering Hops (90 min.)	Grain, 5 Gal.	Extract, 5 Gal.	Grain, 1 Bbl.
Fuggle (4% alpha)	2.00 oz. (68.0 g)	2.00 oz. (68.0 g)	12.40 oz. (3.5 kg)
HBU	4	4	—
IBU	24	24	24

Brewing Specifics

Color:	22 °L
Mash temperature:	150 °F (65.5 °C)
OG:	1.036 (9 °P)
FG:	1.008 (2 °P)
Priming sugar:	2.00 oz. (57.0 g) cane sugar in 5 gal.
CO_2:	1.3 to 2.5 volumes
Packaging:	Draught or nitrogen
Finings:	3.00 oz. isinglass to 5 gal.

Note: This recipe represents the modern dark mild ale. It is something of a collective example, considering all the milds I have tasted and all the mild brewers I have talked to. For an added dimension, try dry-hopping with about 0.25 to 0.50 oz. of Fuggle, Willamette, or Styrian Golding.

Lusty Gnome Midlands Mild

Mash	Grain, 5 Gal.	Extract, 5 Gal.	Grain, 1 Bbl.
Pale malt	11.00 lbs. (5.0 kg)	—	68.20 lbs. (31.0 kg)
Pale malt extract	—	9.00 lbs. (3.6 kg)	—
Crystal malt	3.60 lbs. (1.7 kg)	3.60 lbs. (1.7 kg)	22.30 lbs. (10.0 kg)

Bittering Hops (90 min.)	Grain, 5 Gal.	Extract, 5 Gal.	Grain, 1 Bbl.
Fuggle (4.5% alpha)	1.59 oz. (43.0 g)	1.50 oz. (43.0 g)	9.30 oz. (265.0 g)
Golding (5% alpha)	1.25 oz. (35.0 g)	1.25 oz. (35.0 g)	7.75 oz. (221.0 g)
HBU	13.0	13.0	80.6
IBU	30	30	30

Aroma Hops (15 min.)	Grain, 5 Gal.	Extract, 5 Gal.	Grain, 1 Bbl.
Golding	0.66 oz. (20.0 g)	0.66 oz. (20.0 g)	4.00 oz. (114.0 g)

Brewing Specifics

Color:	10–12 °L
Mash Temperature	155 °F (68 °C)
OG:	1.058 (14.3 °P)
FG:	1.014 (3.6 °P)
Priming sugar	2.00 oz. (57.0 g) cane sugar in 5 gal.
CO_2:	2.0–2.5 volumes
Packaging:	Draught or bottle-conditioned
Finings:	3.00 oz. (85.5 g) isinglass to 5 gal. (If bottled, first add isinglass to a separate vessel, let it drop bright, and then rack the ale into a bottling bucket and bottle.)

Note: Lusty Gnome Midlands Mild is loosely patterned after a higher-gravity mild that is being brewed in the English Midlands today. The gravity is reminiscent of the nineteenth-century milds, and the alcohol content should dispel the myth that milds are supposed to be weak.

Mild Ale, c. 1824

Malt	%	Grain, 5 Gal.	Extract, 5 Gal.	Grain, 1 Bbl.
Mild ale malt	50	6.25 lbs. (2.9 kg)	—	38.75 lbs. (17.7 kg)
Pale malt extract	50	—	7.50 lbs. (3.4 kg)	—
Amber malt[a]	10	20.00 oz. (570.0 g)	20.00 oz. (285.0 g)	7.25 lbs. (3.5 kg)
Caramalt (carapils)	40	5.00 lbs. (2.3 kg)	2.00 lbs. (912.0 g)	31.00 lbs. (14.1 kg)

Bittering Hops (90 min.)	Grain, 5 Gal.	Extract, 5 Gal.	Grain, 1 Bbl.
Golding (4% alpha)	3.33 oz. (95.0 g)	3.33 oz. (95.0 g)	1.25 lbs. (570.0 g)
HBU	13.2	13.2	80.0
IBU	56	56	56

Brewing Specifics

Color:	6–8 °L
Mash temperature:	152 °F (66.5 °C)
OG:	1.066 (16.1 °P)
FG:	1.019 (4.9 °P)
Priming sugar:	2.00 oz. (57.0 g) cane sugar in 5 gal.
CO_2:	1.5–2.0 volumes
Packaging:	Draught or Bottle Conditioned
Finings:	3.00 oz. isinglass to 5 gal. (If bottled, gently stir into bottling bucket.)

[a]Beeston Amber Malt.

Source: Converted from *The Young Brewer's Monitor* (London: 1824).

Producers of
Real Mild Ale
in Great Britain

The following statistics were compiled by the Campaign for Real Ale. The list includes independent British breweries, national concerns, and homebrew pubs.

Brewery	Name of Beer	OG	ABV (%)
Abel Brown's	Lord Douglas Mild	1040	4.0
Adnam's	Mild	1035	3.2
Adnam's	Old	1043	4.3

Appendix A

Brewery	Name of Beer	OG	ABV (%)
Ansells	Mild	1033	3.4
Ballard's	Midhurst Mild	1034	3.5
Banks's	Banks's	1036	3.5
Banks's	Hansons Mild	1035	3.3
Banks and Taylor	Shefford Mild	1038	3.8
Bass (Museum)	No. 6 Mild	1037	3.9
Bass (Museum)	Offilers Mild	1037	3.9
Bass (Sheffield)	Mild	1032	3.1
Bateman's	Mild	1033	3.0
Batham	A J Mild	1049	5.0
Batham	Mild	1037	3.5
Beecham's	Dark Mild	1045	4.5
Bellhaven	60 Shilling	1030	2.9
Blackawton	Dart Mild	1036	3.6
Blackburn	BBC3	1038	3.8
Boddington's	Mild	1032	3.5
Boddington's	OB Mild	1032	3.3

Brewery	Name of Beer	OG	ABV (%)
Boddington's	Pub Ale	1035	3.6
Blue Moon	Dark Side	1041	4.0
Border	Noggin's Nog	1041	4.2
Brains	Dark Mild Ale	1035	3.5
Brakspear	Mild	1031	3.0
Brewery on Sea	Spinnaker Mild	1036	3.5
British Oak	Oak Mild	1038	3.7
Buckley	Buckley's Dark Mild	1035	3.4
Buffy's	Mild	1042	4.2
Bull Mastiff	Ebony dark	1073	7.0
Burtonwood	Dark Mild	1032	3.0
Bushy's	Dark Mild	1035	3.5
Butterknowle	West Auckland Mild	1034	3.3
Cains	Dark Mild	1032	3.2
Caledonian	60 Shilling	1032	3.2
Cannon Royal	Fruiterers Mild	1037	3.7
Church End	Gravediggers Mild	1038	3.8

Brewery	Name of Beer	OG	ABV (%)
Clark (William)	Thistle Mild	1040	4.0
Coach House	Gunpowder Strong Mild	1037	3.8
Cotleigh	Nutcracker Mild	1036	3.6
Crouch Vale	Best Dark Ale	1036	3.6
Cuckmere Haven	Velvet Dark Mild	1048	4.7
Dark Star	Roast Mild	1035	3.5
Davenports Arms	Reynold's Redneck	1056	5.5
Donnington	XXX	1036	3.6
Earl Soham	Gannett Mild	1033	3.0
Easingwold	Tender Mild	1035	3.4
Elgood's	Black Dog Mild	1035	3.6
Enville	High Gravity Mild	1042	4.2
Enville	Low Gravity Mild	1038	3.8
Everards	Mild	1036	3.3
Felinfoel	Dark	1032	3.2

Brewery	Name of Beer	OG	ABV (%)
Fiddler's	Mild	1035	3.4
Firkin Pub Chain	Firkin Mild	1034	3.4
Fox and Hounds	Wild Mild	1043	4.2
Gale's	Festival Mild	1052	4.8
Goacher's	Real Mild Ale	1033	3.4
Greenall Whitley	Greenalls Mild	1032	3.3
Greene King	Black Baron	1044	4.3
Greene King	XX Dark Mild	1036	3.0
Green Jack	Mild	1032	3.0
Guernsey	Braye	1038	3.7
Hanby	Black Magic Mild	1033	3.3
Hardy's and Hansons	Kimberley Best Mild	1035	3.1
Harveys	Knots of May	1030	3.0
Harveys	Sussex XX Mild Ale	1030	3.0
Highgate and Walsall	Dark Mild	1035	3.2

Brewery	Name of Beer	OG	ABV (%)
Hogsback	Dark Mild	1036	3.4
Holden's	Mild	1037	3.7
Holt	Mild	1032	3.2
Holt, Plant and Deakin	Holts Mild	1036	3.7
Home	Mild	1036	3.6
Hook Norton	PAB Mild	1031	3.0
Hoskins and Oldfield	HOB Best Mild	1036	3.5
Hughes (Sarah Hughes)	Dark Ruby Mild	1058	6.0
Hull	Mild	1034	3.3
Hyde's Anvil	Dark Mild	1032	3.5
Hyde's Anvil	Mild	1032	3.5
Isle of Man (Okells)	Mild	1034	3.4
Jennings	Dark Mild	1031	3.1
Joshua Tetley	Pale Mild	1032	3.3
Joshua Tetlley	Dark Mild	1032	3.2

Real Mild Ale in Great Britain

Brewery	Name of Beer	OG	ABV (%)
Kelham Island	Bête Noire	1056	5.5
King and Barnes	Mild Ale	1034	3.5
Leatherbritches	Scrum Down Mild	1053	5.0
Leatherbritches	Steaming Billy Mild	1038	3.0
Lees	GB Mild	1033	3.5
Leyland	Old Cock Up Mild	1032	3.5
Linfit	Dark Mild	1032	3.0
Little Avenham	Arkwright Mild	1035	3.5
McGuiness	Feather Plucker Mild	1034	4.0
McMullen	Original AK	1033	3.7
Malton	Dark	1035	3.5
Mansfield	Gray's Mild	1035	3.5
Mansfield	Riding Mild	1035	3.5
Marston, Thompson, and Evershed	Walnut Mild	1035	3.5
Mathew Brown	Lion Mild	1030	3.1

Appendix A

Brewery	Name of Beer	OG	ABV (%)
Mitchell and Butlers	M & B Mild	1034.5	3.2
Mitchell's	Country Mild	1035	3.3
Moorehouses	Black Cat Mild	1034	3.2
Morrell's	Oxford Mild	1039	3.7
Old Chimneys	Military Mild	1035	3.4
Old Court (Whitbread)	Copper's Ale	1034	3.4
Old Mill	Traditional Mild	1035	3.4
Parish	Mild	1035	3.5
Pembroke	The Darklin	1035	3.5
Phoenix	Mild	1040	4.0
Porter	Dark Mild	1033	3.3
Reepham	Strong Ruby Ale	1048	4.5
Reindeer	Mild	1034	3.4
Ridley's	Champion Mild	1035	3.5
Riverhead	Sparth Mild	1036	3.6
Robinson's	Dark Best Mild	1033	3.3

Brewery	Name of Beer	OG	ABV (%)
Robinson's	Hatters Mild	1033	3.3
Rudgate	Ruby Mild	1041	4.4
Ryburn	Best Mild	1033	3.3
Scott's	Strong Mild	1043	4.4
Shipstones	Mild	1034	3.4
St. Austell	XXXX Mild	1039	3.6
St. Peter's	Mild	1035	3.6
Tally Ho!	Master Jack Mild	1039	3.5
Theakston	Traditional Mild	1035	3.5
Three Tuns	Dark Mild	1034	3.4
Thwaites	Best Mild	1034	3.3
Timothy Taylor	Dark Mild	1034	3.5
Timothy Taylor	Golden Best	1033	3.5
Titanic	Lifeboat Ale	1040	3.9
Tolly Cobbold	Mild	1032	3.2
Tomlinson's	Hermitage Mild	1036	3.7
Ventnor	Dark Mild	1033	3.3

Appendix A

Brewery	Name of Beer	OG	ABV (%)
Viking	Island Dark Mild	1035	3.5
Ward's	Darley's Dark Mild	1034	3.4
Webster's	Green Label	1032	3.2
Welsh Brewer's	Worthington Dark	1034.5	3.2
Whim	Magic Mushroom Mild	1042	3.8
Wilsons	Original Mild	1032	3.0
Winfields	Mild	1035	3.5
Woodforde's	Mardler's Mild	1035	3.5

Further Reading

Perhaps the biggest reason that mild ale has not enjoyed the success that other beers have in these times of revivalist brewing is because there is so little information available about the style. The books listed in this appendix cover a wide range of brewing topics and range from antiquated brewing texts to volumes on general modern brewing knowledge and historical works that put mild ale into perspective. If you have consulted any of the footnotes to this book, you will no doubt recognize many of these titles.

Brewing Texts

Clissold, Ivor. *Cellarmanship: Caring for Real Ale*. St. Albans, Hertfordshire, U.K.: CAMRA Ltd., 1997.

Daniels, Ray. *Designing Great Beers: The Ultimate Guide to Brewing Classic Beer Styles*. Boulder, Colo.: Brewers Publications, 1996.

———. *The Perfect Pint: Producing Real Ale in America*. Chicago: Craft Beer Institute, 1998.

Daniels, Ray, and Jim Parker. *Brown Ale: History, Brewing Techniques, Recipes*. Boulder, Colo.: Brewers Publications, 1998.

DeClerck, Jean. *A Textbook of Brewing*. Translated by Kathleen Barton-Wright. 1957; reprinted by the Siebel Institute of Technology, Chicago, 1994.

Foster, Terry. *Pale Ale*. Classic Beer Style Series, no. 1. Boulder, Colo.: Brewers Publications, 1990.

———. *Porter*. Classic Beer Style Series, no. 5. Boulder, Colo.: Brewers Publications, 1992.

Hind, H. Lloyd. *Brewing Science and Practice*. New York: John Wiley and Sons, 1943.

Lewis, Michael J., and Tom W. Young. *Brewing*. London: Chapman and Hall, 1995.

Noonan, Gregory J. *New Brewing Lager Beer*. Boulder, Colo.: Brewers Publications, 1996.

———. *Scotch Ale*. Classic Beer Style Series, no. 8. Boulder, Colo.: Brewers Publications, 1996.

Historical Sources

Bradley, Richard. *A Guide to Gentleman Farmers and Housekeepers for Brewing the Finest Malt Liquors.* 1700; reprint 1997, Birch Run Press, Richfield, Ohio.

Briggs, D. E., J. S. Hough, and T. W. Young, eds. *Malting and Brewing Science,* 2nd ed. London: Chapman and Hall, 1981.

Glover, Brian. *Prince of Ales.* St. Albans, Hertfordshire, U.K.: CAMRA Ltd., 1993.

Gourvish, T. R. *The British Brewing Industry 1830–1980.* Cambridge, U.K.: Cambridge University Press, 1994.

Harrison, John. *Old British Beers and How to Make Them.* London: Durden Park Beer Circle, 1991.

Jackson, Michael. *Michael Jackson's Beer Companion,* 2nd ed. Philadelphia: Running Press, 1997.

Mathias, Peter. *The Brewing Industry in England: 1700–1830.* Brookfield, Vt.: Gregg Revivals, 1993.

Protz, Roger. *The Ale Trail.* St. Albans, Hertfordshire, U.K.: Verulam Publishing, 1995.

Sambrook, Pamela. *Country House Brewing in England: 1500–1900.* London: Hambledon Press, 1996.

Tuck, John. *Private Brewers Guide to the Art of Brewing Ale and Porter.* 1882; reprinted by Zymoscribe, Woodbridge, Conn., 1995.

Useful Information

TABLE 1

Solubility of CO_2 at Atmospheric Pressure

°C	Volumes CO_2	°F	Volumes CO_2
0	1.70	32	1.70
2	1.60	35	1.60
4	1.50	40	1.45
6	1.40	45	1.30
8	1.30	50	1.20
10	1.20	55	1.10
12	1.12	60	1.00
14	1.05	65	0.92
16	0.99	70	0.85
18	0.93	75	0.78
20	0.88		
22	0.83		

TABLE 2

Volumes of CO_2 at Various Temperatures and Pressures

Temp.		Volumes of CO_2 at Given Temperature and Pressure											
°F	°C	5 psi	7	9	11	13	15	17	19	21	23	25	27
32	0	2.15	2.38	2.59	2.80	3.00	3.21						
35	1.7	2.02	2.24	2.43	2.63	2.83	3.02	3.22					
40	4.0	1.83	2.01	2.20	2.39	2.56	2.75	2.93	3.10	3.28			
45	7.2	1.66	1.84	2.00	2.17	2.34	2.51	2.69	2.86	3.02	3.19		
50	10.0	1.50	1.66	1.82	1.98	2.14	2.30	2.46	2.62	2.78	2.94	3.10	
52			1.61	1.76	1.92	2.06	2.22	2.38	2.53	2.68	2.84	3.00	3.13
54			1.56	1.71	1.86	2.00	2.15	2.30	2.45	2.59	2.74	2.89	3.04
56			1.50	1.65	1.79	1.93	2.08	2.22	2.36	2.50	2.64	2.78	2.92
58				1.59	1.74	1.87	2.01	2.15	2.28	2.42	2.55	2.69	2.82
60	15.6			1.54	1.69	1.82	1.95	2.08	2.21	2.34	2.47	2.60	2.73
62					1.63	1.76	1.88	2.01	2.14	2.26	2.39	2.52	2.64
64					1.58	1.70	1.82	1.94	2.06	2.18	2.30	2.43	2.55
66					1.52	1.64	1.76	1.88	1.99	2.11	2.23	2.35	2.47

Source: Data taken from *Methods of Analysis*, 5th ed. (Milwaukee, Wis.: The American Society of Brewing Chemists, 1949).

Useful Temperature Conversions

To convert °Celsius to °Fahrenheit, multiply by 9, divide by 5, then add 32.

To convert °Fahrenheit to °Celsius, subtract 32, then multiply by 5 and divide by 9.

To convert °Reaumur to °Celsius, multiply by 5 and divide by 4.

To convert °Celsius to °Reaumur, multiply by 4 and divide by 5.

To convert °Reaumur to °Fahrenheit, multiply by 9, divide by 4, then subtract 32.

To convert °Fahrenheit to °Reaumur, subtract 32 then multiply
   by 4 and divide by 9.

Useful Measurement Conversions

1 imperial (U.K.) barrel = 2 kilderkins = 4 firkins = 36 gallons
   = 1.6356 hl = 1.4 U.S. barrels

1 imperial (U.K.) pint = 20 fl. oz. = .5682 liter = 28.412 ml

1 imperial (U.K.) gallon = 160 fl. oz. = 8 pints = 10 lb. = 1.201
   U.S. gallons = 4.546 liters

1 U.S. barrel = 31 U.S. gallons = 25.81 imperial (U.K.) gallons
   = 1.1734 hl = .717 imperial barrel

1 U.S. gallon = 128 fl. oz. = 8 U.S. pints = 3.7853 liters
   = .8327 imperial (U.K.) gallon

1 oz. = 64.8 mg

1 lb. = 16 oz. = 256 drams = .45359 kg

Britain

1 bushel barley = 56 lb. = 25.401 kg

1 quarter barley = 448 lb. = 203.209 kg

1 bushel malt = 42 lb. = 19.051 kg

1 quarter malt = 336 lb. = 152.407 kg

United States

1 bushel barley = 48 lb.

1 bushel malt = 34 lb.

Appendix C

TABLE 3

Short Table for Converting Specific Gravity at 20 °C to °Plato

SG	°P	SG	°P	SG	°P
1000	0.00	1030	7.56	1060	14.75
1001	0.26	1031	7.80	1061	14.98
1002	0.52	1032	8.05	1062	15.21
1003	0.78	1033	8.29	1063	15.44
1004	1.03	1034	8.54	1064	15.68
1005	1.29	1035	8.87	1065	15.91
1006	1.54	1036	9.03	1066	16.14
1007	1.80	1037	9.27	1067	16.37
1008	2.05	1038	9.51	1068	16.60
1009	2.31	1039	9.75	1069	16.83
1010	2.56	1040	10.00	1070	17.06
1011	2.82	1041	10.24	1071	17.29
1012	3.07	1042	10.48	1072	17.52
1013	3.32	1043	10.72	1073	17.74
1014	3.58	1044	10.96	1074	17.97
1015	3.83	1045	11.20	1075	18.20
1016	4.08	1046	11.44	1076	18.43
1017	4.33	1047	11.68	1077	18.65
1018	4.58	1048	11.92	1078	18.88
1019	5.08	1049	12.15	1079	19.11
1020	5.33	1050	12.39	1080	19.33
1021	5.58	1051	12.63	1081	19.55
1022	5.83	1052	12.87	1082	19.78
1023	6.08	1053	13.10	1083	20.00
1024	6.33	1054	13.34	1084	20.23
1025	6.57	1055	13.57	1085	20.45
1026	6.82	1056	13.81	1086	20.67
1027	7.07	1057	14.04	1087	20.90
1028	7.31	1058	14.28	1088	21.12
1029	7.56	1059	14.51	1089	21.34

Note: As a quick conversion that is more or less accurate up to SG 1060, divide the last two digits of a SG reading by 4 to get approximate °Plato or °Balling. Conversely, multiply °Plato or °Balling by 4 to get approximate SG.

Chapter Notes

Introduction

1. Charlie Papazian, *The New Complete Joy of Homebrewing*, 2nd Edition (New York: Avon Books, 1991), 141.
2. Roger Protz, *The Ale Trail* (London: CAMRA Publications, 1996), 148. CAMRA is the Campaign for Real Ale.
3. Michael Jackson, *Michael Jackson's Beer Companion*, 2nd Edition (Philadelphia: Running Press, 1997), 74.

Chapter 1. Mild Ale: The Historical Perspective

1. Roger Protz, *The Ale Trail* (London: CAMRA Publications, 1996).
2. Ibid.
3. Ibid.
4. W. Young, *The New and True Art of Brewing* (London: St. Paul's Churchyard, 1692; reprint, Richfield, Ohio: Birch Run Press, n.d.), 18.
5. Michael Jackson, *The Beer Companion* (Philadelphia: Running Press, 1993), 14.
6. Dr. John Harrison, *Old British Beers and How to Make Them* (Wiltshire, U.K.: Durden Park Beer Circle, 1991), 7.
7. Brian Glover, *The Prince of Ales: The History of Brewing in Wales* (Phoenix Mill, London: Allan Sutton Publishing, 1993), 1.

8. E. Hughes, *A Treatise on the Brewing of Beer* (1796; reprint, Richfield, Ohio: Birch Run Press, 1997).

9. Terry Foster, *Porter* (Boulder: Brewers Publications, 1992), 6.

10. Roger Protz, personal communication (November 1997).

11. Richard Bradley, *A Guide to Gentleman Farmers and House-keepers for Brewing the Finest Malt Liquors* (1700; reprint, Richfield, Ohio: Birch Run Press, 1997).

12. Ibid.

13. Jackson, *The Beer Companion*, 21.

14. John Tuck, *The Private Brewer's Guide to the Art of Brewing Ale and Porter* (London: 1822; reprint, Woodbridge, Conn.: ZymoScribe, 1995), 3–4, 128, 170.

15. César de Saussure (November 29, 1726), from *A Foreign View of England* (1902), 158, as quoted in Peter Mathias, *The Brewing Industry in England 1700–1830* (Cambridge, U.K.: Cambridge University Press, 1959), 14.

16. Truman Brewing Company's Records, manuscript (1802).

17. *Journal of the House of Commons*, XXIV (n.d.), 541–542.

18. Mathias, *The Brewing Industry in England,* 58.

19. Ibid., 62.

20. David Wheeler, *British Patent No. 4112* (1817).

21. Michael Lewis, *Stout* (Boulder: Brewers Publications, 1995).

22. T. R. Gourvish and R. G. Wilson, *The British Brewing Industry 1830–1980* (Cambridge, U.K.: Cambridge University Press, 1994).

23. Foster, *Porter*.

24. Select Committee of the House of Commons on the Sale of Beer, Q3906, 230, as quoted in Gourvish and Wilson, *The British Brewing Industry,* 42.

25. *Licensed Victuallers' Gazette* (December 4, 1875).
26. Alfred Barnard, *Noted Breweries of Great Britain and Ireland, Vol. I* (1889), 378.
27. F. Faulkner, *The Art of Brewing* (London: 1875), 43–44.
28. J. L. Baker, *The Brewing Industry* (London: 1905), 11–12
29. E. A. Pratt, *The Licensed Trade: An Independent Survey* (1909), 229–241
30. *Licensed Victuallers' Gazette* (October 9, 1875).
31. Gourvish and Wilson, *The British Brewing Industry,* 38–41.
32. R. Wahl and M. Henius, *The American Handy-Book of Brewing, Malting and Auxiliary Trades* (Chicago: Wahl-Henius Institute, 1908), 1251–1253
33. H. Lloyd Hind, *Brewing Science and Practice* (London: Chapman & Hall, Ltd., 1940), 394–395.
34. Gourvish and Wilson, *The British Brewing Industry,* 558.
35. Ibid.

Chapter 2. The Flavor Profile of Mild Ale

1. Ray Daniels, *Designing Great Beers* (Boulder: Brewers Publications, 1996), 221.
2. Roger Protz, *A Beer Drinker's Almanac* (London: CAMRA Publications).

Chapter 3. Mild Ale Ingredients

1. Michael Lewis, *Stout* (Boulder: Brewers Publications, 1995), 44.
2. Michael Jackson, *Michael Jackson's Beer Companion*, 2nd Edition (Philadelphia: Running Press, 1997).+
3. W. R. Loftus, *The Brewer* (London: c. 1850).
4. Ibid.

5. D. E. Briggs, J. S. Hough, R. Stevens, and T. W. Young, *Malting and Brewing Science*, Volume 1 (London: Chapman, Hall, 1981), 223.

6. Andrew Walsh, "The Mark of Nobility," *Brewing Techniques* 6, no. 2 (March–April 1998).

7. Gregory Noonan, *Scotch Ale* (Boulder: Brewers Publications, 1993), 52.

Chapter 4. Brewing Equipment and Methods

1. Dr. John Harrison, *Old English Beers and How to Make Them* (London: The Durden Park Beer Circle, 1992).

2. Ibid.

Chapter 6. Commercially Produced Mild Ales

1. Michael Jackson, *Michael Jackson's Beer Companion*, 2nd Edition (Philadelphia: Running Press, 1997), 71.

Glossary

acrospire. The germinal plant-growth of the barley kernel.

adjunct. Any unmalted grain or other fermentable ingredient added to the mash.

adjuncts. Sources of fermentable extract other than malted barley. Principally corn, rice, wheat, unmalted barley, and glucose (dextrose).

aerate. To force atmospheric air or oxygen into solution. Introducing air to the wort at various stages of the brewing process.

aeration. The action of introducing air to the wort at various stages of the brewing process.

aerobic. In the presence of or requiring oxygen.

airlock. *See* fermentation lock.

airspace. *See* ullage.

AK. An early stylistic designation for relatively low-gravity pale beers, many of which were described as pale milds. Only a very few breweries still manufacture products known as AK.

albumin. Intermediate soluble protein that is subject to coagulation upon heating. Hydrolyzed to peptides and amino acids by proteolytic enzymes.

alcohol by volume (ABV). The percentage of volume of alcohol per volume of beer. To calculate the approximate volumetric alcohol content, subtract the final gravity (FG) from the original gravity (OG) and divide the result by 75. For example: 1.050 – 1.012 = 0.038 / 0.0075 = 5% ABV.

alcohol by weight (ABW). The percentage weight of alcohol per volume of beer. For example, 3.2% alcohol by weight = 3.2 grams of alcohol per 100 centiliters of beer. Alcohol by weight can be converted to alcohol by volume by multiplying by 0.795.

ale. 1. Historically, an unhopped malt beverage. 2. Now, a generic term for hopped beers produced by top fermentation, as opposed to lagers, which are produced by bottom fermentation. 3. Once used as a catch-all term to describe British beers that were neither "pale" or "old" and thus "mild."

all-extract beer. A beer made with only malt extract, as opposed to one made from barley or a combination of malt extract and barley.

all-grain beer. A beer made with only malted barley, as opposed to one made from malt extract or from malt extract and malted barley.

alpha-acid unit (AAU). The number of AAUs in a hop addition is equal to the weight of the addition in ounces times the alpha-acid percentage. Thus 1 ounce of 5% alpha-acid hops contains 5 AAUs. AAU is the same as homebrewers' bittering units.

alpha acid (a-acid). The principle source of bitterness from hops when isomerized by boiling. These separate but related alpha acids come from the soft alpha resin of the hop. (When boiled, alpha acids are converted to iso-alpha-acids.)

ambient temperature. The surrounding temperature.

amino acids. The building blocks of proteins. Essential components of wort, these acids are required for adequate yeast growth.

anaerobic. Conditions under which there is not enough oxygen for respiratory metabolic function. Anaerobic microorganisms are those that can function without the presence of free molecular oxygen.

apparent attenuation. A simple measure of the extent of fermentation that a wort has undergone in the process of becoming beer. Using gravity units (GU), Balling (B), or Plato (P) units to express gravity, apparent attenuation is equal to the original gravity (OG) minus the terminal gravity divided by the OG. The result is expressed as a percentage and equals 65 to 80% for most beers.

apparent extract. The terminal gravity of a beer.

aqueous. Consisting of or comprising water.

attemper. To regulate or modify the temperature.

attemperator. A device used to regulate or modify the temperature of fermenting or aging beer in traditional British breweries. Usually composed of a network of tubing carrying water or some other refrigerated liquid immersed in the beer.

attenuate. To reduce the extract/density by yeast metabolism.

attenuation. The reduction in the wort's specific gravity caused by the transformation of sugars into ethanol and carbon-dioxide gas.

autolysis. Yeast death due to shock or nutrient-depleted solutions.

bacteriostatic. Bacteria inhibiting.

Balling (°B). A saccharometer invented by Carl Joseph Napoleon Balling in 1843. A standard for the measurement of the density of solutions. It is calibrated for 63.5 °F (17.5 °C), and graduated in grams per 100, giving a direct reading of the percentage of extract by weight per 100 grams solution. For example, 10 °B = 10 grams of cane sugar per 100 grams of solution.

barrel. 1. The prevailing unit of measurement in both the British and U.S. brewing industries, equal to 31 U.S. gallons for a U.S. barrel and 36 imperial (U.K.) gallons for an imperial barrel. 2. A cask used in the dispense of real ale that holds 36 imperial (U.K.) gallons or 43.2 U.S. gallons.

bbl. Abbreviation for beer barrel. *See* barrel.

beer engine. A hand-operated pump for pulling beer from casks in the pub cellar to the pub bar.

beerstone. Brownish-gray mineral-like deposits left on fermentation equipment that is composed of calcium oxalate and organic residues.

blow-off. A single-stage homebrewing fermentation method in which a plastic tube is fitted into the mouth of a carboy, with the other end submerged in a pail of sterile water. Unwanted residues and carbon dioxide are expelled through the tube, while air is prevented from coming into contact with the fermenting beer, thus avoiding contamination.

body. A qualitative indicator of the fullness or mouthfeel of a beer. Related to the proportion of unfermentable long-chain sugars or dextrins present in the beer.

Brettanomyces. A genus of yeasts that have a role in the production of some beers, such as modern *lambics* and Berliner *weisse* and historical porters.

brewer's gravity (SG). *See* gravity.

BU:GU ratio. The ratio of bitterness units (BU) to gravity units (GU) for a specific beer or group of beers. International bitterness units (IBU) are used for bitterness, and gravity units (GU) are used for the gravity component. GU = original gravity − 1 × 1,000. For most beers and beer styles, the resulting ratio has a value between 0.3 and 1.0.

buffer. A substance capable of resisting changes in the pH of a solution.

Burton Union. A once-popular method of fermentation in small (3-barrel) oaken barrels connected by a network of piping. The method was prevelent in Burton-on-Trent and elsewhere, but it is now very rare.

carbonates. Alkaline salts whose anions are derived from carbonic acid.

carbonation. The process of introducing carbon-dioxide gas into a liquid by (1) injecting the finished beer with carbon dioxide; (2) adding young fermenting beer to finished beer for a renewed fermentation (kraeusening); (3) priming (adding sugar or wort) to fermented wort prior to bottling, thereby creating a secondary fermentation in the bottle; or (4) finishing fermentation under pressure.

carboy. A large glass, plastic, or earthenware bottle.

caryophylline. A secondary component of hop oil found in varying proportions in different varieties of hops.

cellulose. A polymer of sugar molecules that plays a structural rather than a storage role. The sugars that make up cellulose cannot be liberated by the enzymes found in most plant systems.

chill haze. Haziness caused by protein and tannin during the secondary fermentation.

chillproof. Cold-conditioning to precipitate chill haze.

cleanse. To cause beer to become bright, often used in reference to fermentation methods such as the Burton Union system and the Yorkshire squares system.

closed fermentation. Fermentation under closed, anaerobic conditions to minimize risk of contamination and oxidation.

coliform. Waterborne bacteria, often associated with pollution.

cylindro-conical fermenter. A fermentation tank consisting of a cylindrical tank with a conical bottom for easily harvesting yeast. It is the most common type of fermenter in the United States.

decoction. Boiling to extract the flavor and facilitate the degradation of starches and proteins; the part of the mash that is boiled.

density. The measurement of the weight of a given solution, as compared to the weight of an equal volume of pure water.

dextrin. Soluble polysaccharide fraction from the hydrolysis of starch by heat, acid, or enzyme.

diacetyl. *See* diketone.

diacetyl rest. A warm—55 to 70 °F (13 to 21 °C)—rest that occurs during fermentation. During the diacetyl rest, yeast metabolizes diacetyl and other byproducts of fermentation.

diastase. Starch-reducing enzymes. Usually alpha- and beta-amylase, but also limit dextrinase and a-glucosidase (maltase).

diastatic malt extract. A type of malt extract containing the diastatic enzymes naturally found in malt and needed for conversion of starch into sugar. This type of extract is sometimes used in recipes that contain grain adjuncts such as corn or rice.

diketone. A class of aromatic, volatile compounds perceivable in minute concentrations from yeast or *Pediococcus* bacteria metabolism—most significantly, the butter and butterscotch aroma of diacetyl, a vicinal diketone (VDK). The other significant compound relevant to brewing is 2,3-pentanedione.

dimethyl sulfide (DMS). An important sulfur-carrying compound originating in malt. Adds a crisp, "lager-like" character at low levels and corn or cabbage flavors at high levels.

disaccharides. A sugar group; two monosaccharide molecules joined by the removal of a water molecule.

drop. 1. To transfer beer from one bulk vessel to another by means of gravity. 2. To become clear and refined, as in to "drop bright" by means of natural sedimentation or through the use of finings.

dry hopping. The addition of hops to the primary fermenter, the secondary fermenter, or to casked beer to add aroma and hop character to the finished beer without adding significant bitterness.

dry malt. Malt extract in powdered form.

European Brewery Convention (EBC). *See* SRM.

enzymes. Protein-based organic catalysts that affect changes in the compositions of the substances on which they act.

essential oil. The aromatic, volatile compounds from the hop.

ester. A class of organic compounds created from the reaction of an alcohol and an organic acid. They tend to have fruity aromas and are detectable at low concentrations.

esters. "Ethereal salts," such as ethyl acetate. Aromatic compounds from fermentation composed of an acid and an alcohol, such as the "banana" ester. Formed by yeast enzymes from an alcohol and an acid. Associated with ale and high-temperature fermentations, esters also arise to some extent with pure lager yeast cultures, though more so with low wort oxygenation, high initial fermentation temperatures, and high-gravity wort. Top-fermenting yeast strains are prized for their ability to produce particular mixes of esters.

extract. The amount of dissolved materials in the wort after mashing and lautering malted barley and/or malt adjuncts such as corn and rice.

extraction. Drawing out the soluble essence of the malt or hops.

fermentation lock. A one-way valve that allows carbon-dioxide gas to escape from the fermenter while excluding contaminants.

final specific gravity. The specific gravity of a beer when fermentation is complete.

fining. (n.) A clarifying agent. (v.) The process of adding clarifying agents to beer during secondary fermentation to precipitate suspended matter. Examples of clarifying agents are isinglass, gelatin, bentonite, silica gel, or polyvinyl pyrrolidone.

firkin. A cask used to dispense real ale that holds 9 imperial (U.K.) gallons or 10.8 U.S. gallons. It is the most common size of cask in the British and the emerging U.S. real ale market.

flocculation. The tendency of yeast to clump together at the end of fermentation. The greater the tendency for the yeast to flocculate, the faster it will drop out of the solution, thereby creating clearer or brighter beer.

germination. Sprouting the barley kernel to initiate enzyme development and conversion of the malt.

glucophilic. An organism that thrives on glucose.

gravity (SG). Specific gravity as expressed by brewers. For example, specific gravity 1.046 is expressed as SG 1046. Density of a solution as compared to water; expressed in grams per milliliter (1 milliliter of water weighs 1 gram, hence a specific gravity of 1.000 = SG 1000; specific gravity of. 1.046 = SG 1046).

gravity units (GU). A form of expressing specific gravity in formulas as a whole number. It is equal to the significant digits to the right of the decimal point (1.055 SG becomes 55 GU, and 1.108 SG becomes 108 GU).

green malt. Malt that has been steeped and germinated and is ready for kilning.

gruit. A mixture of spices and herbs used to bitter and flavor ales before hops became accepted as a bittering and flavoring agent.

gyle. A single wort drawn from a mash. Can refer to one of several successively weaker worts, as in "parti-gyle," or to one wort drawn from a mash, as in "single-gyle." *See* parti-gyle.

heat. Arcane word for temperature. "The correct heat in the first wetting the malt, stamps the character of the whole gyle, the heat most adapted to open the pores of the grain must be correct, and after that is done, a higher heat can be added, without prejudicee to the flavour of the Wort, a rich flavour of the Malt, is what we seek to obtain in the beer." (From George Stewart Amsinck, *Practical Brewings: A Series of Fifty Brewings*.)

hemocytometer. A device used for counting blood cells (or brewer's yeast) under a microscope.

hexose. Sugar molecules of six carbon atoms. Includes glucose, fructose, lactose, mannose, and galactose.

hogshead. A cask used in the dispense of real ale that holds 54 imperial (U.K.) gallons or 64.8 U.S. gallons.

homebrew bittering unit (HBU). A formula adopted by the American Homebrewers Association to measure the bitterness of beer. For example, 1.5 ounces of hops at 10% alpha acid for 5 gallons: $1.5 \times 10 = 15$ HBU per 5 gallons. Same as alpha-acid unit (AAU).

homofermentive. Organisms that metabolize only one specific carbon source.

hop back. A piece of brew-house equipment designed to separate the trub from the wort after boiling by running the entire wort through a filter bed of fresh hop cones, thereby imparting a unique hop character.

hop pellets. Hop cones compressed into tablets. Hop pellets are 20 to 30% more bitter by weight than the same hop variety in loose form. Hop pellets are less subject to alpha-acid losses than are whole hops.

hydrolysis. Decomposition of matter into soluble fractions by either acids or enzymes in water.

hydrometer. A glass instrument used to measure the specific gravity of liquids as compared to water, consisting of a graduated stem resting on a weighted float.

hydroxide. A compound, usually alkaline, containing the OH (hydroxyl) group.

inoculate. The introduction of a microbe into surroundings capable of supporting its growth.

international bitterness unit (IBU). This is a standard unit that measures the concentration of iso-alpha-acids in milligrams per liter (parts per million). Most procedures will also measure a small amount of uncharacterized soft resins, so IBUs are generally 5 to 15% higher than iso-alpha-acid concentrations.

isinglass. A gelatinous substance made from the swim bladder of certain fish and added to beer as a fining agent.

isomer (ISO). Organic compounds of identical composition and molecular weight but having a different molecular structure.

kilderkin. A cask used in the dispense of real ale that holds 18 imperial (U.K.) gallons or 21.6 U.S. gallons.

kilning. The final stage in the malting of barley that prepares it for use by the brewer. Kilning reduces the moisture contained in the grain to approximately 4% and roasts the malt to some extent. The degree of roasting affects the flavor and color of the malt as well as of the beer it produces.

kraeusen. (n.) The rocky head of foam that appears on the surface of the wort during fermentation. Also used to describe the period of fermentation characterized by a rich foam head. (v.) To add fermenting wort to fermented beer to induce carbonation through a secondary fermentation.

Lactobacillus. Species of bacteria that ferments wort sugars to produce lactic acid. Although considered undesirable in most breweries and beer styles, it plays a significant role in the production of some beers, such as Berliner *weisse* and *lambics*.

lactophilic. An organism that metabolizes lactate more readily than glucose.

lager. (n.) A generic term for any bottom-fermented beer. Lager brewing is now the predominant brewing method worldwide except in Britain, where top-fermented ales dominate. (v.) To store beer at near-freezing temperatures in order to precipitate yeast cells and proteins and improve taste.

lauter. The process of separating the clear liquid from the spent grain and husks.

lauter tun. A vessel in which the mash settles and the grains are removed from the sweet wort through a straining process. It has a false slotted bottom and a spigot.

lipids. Fatlike substances, especially triacylglycerols and fatty acids. Negatively affect a beer's ability to form a foam head. Lipids cause soapy flavors and, when oxidized, contribute stale flavors.

liquefaction. The process by which alpha-amylase enzymes degrade soluble starch into dextrin.

malt. Barley that has been steeped in water, germinated, and then dried in kilns. This process converts insoluble starches to soluble substances and sugars.

malt extract. A thick syrup or dry powder prepared from malt.

maltose. A disaccharide composed of two glucose molecules. The primary sugar obtained by diastatic hydrolysis of starch. One-third the sweetness of sucrose.

mashing. Mixing ground malt with water to extract the fermentables, degrade haze-forming proteins, and convert grain starches to fermentable sugars and nonfermentable carbohydrates.

melanoidins. Color-producing compounds produced through a long series of chemical reactions that begin with the combination of a sugar and an amino acid.

Midlands. A district of England south of Manchester (centered in Wolverhampton) known for its mining and steel industry. The largest area of mild ale popularity.

mild. 1. A British ale of low gravity and low alcoholic strength, either pale or brown in color. 2. Historically, a beer that has not undergone a long aging process or that does not exhibit the characteristic sour and tart flavors associated with long aging in unlined wood. 3. Sometimes used to denote beers with a relatively low hop profile and low alcoholic strength.

modification. 1. The physical and chemical changes that occur in barley during malting where complex molecules are broken down to simpler, soluble molecules. 2. The degree to which malt has undergone these changes, as determined by the growth of the acrospire. The greater the degree of modification, the more readily available starch is and the lower the protein level is.

mole. A unit of measure for chemical compounds. The amount of a substance that has a weight in grams numerically equal to the molecular weight of the substance. Also, gram-molecular weight.

myrcene. A primary component of the essential oil of the hop cone. Although rarely found in beer in this native form, it is processed into a number of flavor-active compounds that are significant in beer. The quantity of myrcene found in a hop varies by variety, year, and growing region.

open fermentation. Prevailing system of fermentation in independent British breweries where beer is fermented in open-to-air wooden, steel, stainless steel, or copper vessels.

original gravity. The specific gravity of wort previous to fermentation. A measure of the total amount of dissolved solids in wort.

oxidation. 1. The combining of oxygen with other molecules, often causing off-flavors, as with oxidized alcohols, to form aldehydes. 2. A reaction in which the atoms in an element lose electrons and its valence is correspondingly increased (oxidation-reduction reaction).

parti-gyle. An arcane system of brewing in which the first runnings of wort are taken to make a high-gravity beer and the grain is then remashed to create another brew. This can be done yet again to make a third brew, all from the same grains. There is usually no sparging involved when using the parti-gyle system. With the advent of more-sophisticated equipment that allowed lautering and sparging, the parti-gyle system of brewing lost favor around the end of the nineteenth century.

pectin. A vegetable substance (a chain of galacturonic acid) that becomes gelatinous in the presence of sugars and acids.

pentosan. Pentose-based complex carbohydrates, especially gums.

pentose. Sugar molecules containing five carbon atoms. Monosaccharides.

peptonizing. The action of proteolytic enzymes upon protein, successively yielding albumin/proteoses, peptides, and amino acids.

pH. A measure of acidity or alkalinity of a solution, usually on a scale of 1 to 14, where 7 is neutral.

phenols. Aromatic hydroxyl precursors of tannins/polyphenols. "Phenolic" in beer describes medicinal flavors from tannins, bacterial growth, cleaning compounds, or plastics.

phosphate. A salt or ester of phosphoric acid.

pitching. Inoculating sterile wort with a vigorous yeast culture.

pin. A cask used in the dispense of real ale that holds 4.5 imperial (U.K.) gallons or 5.4 U.S. gallons. Although they are a perfect size for homebrew use, pins are becoming increasingly rare.

Plato, degrees. Commercial brewers' standard for the measurement of the density of solutions, expressed as the equivalent weight of cane sugar in solution (calibrated on grams of sucrose per 100 grams of solution). Like degrees Balling (°B), but degrees Plato (°P) computations are more exact.

Plato saccharometer. A saccharometer that expresses specific gravity as extract weight in a 100-gram solution at 68 °F (20 °C). A revised, more-accurate version of Balling, developed by Dr. Plato.

polymer. A compound molecule formed by the joining of many smaller identical units. For example, polyphenols are joined phenols, and polypeptides are joined peptides.

polyphenol. Complexes of phenolic compounds involved in chill-haze formation and oxidative staling.

polysaccharides. Carbohydrate complexes that can be reduced to monosaccharides by hydrolysis.

ppm. Parts per million. Equal to milligrams per liter (mg/l). The measurement of particles of matter in solution.

precipitation. Separation of suspended matter by sedimentation.

precursor. The starting materials or inputs for a chemical reaction.

primary fermentation. The first stage of fermentation, during which most fermentable sugars are converted to ethyl alcohol and carbon dioxide.

priming. The act of adding priming sugar to a still (or flat) beer so that it may develop carbonation.

priming solution. A solution of sugar in water added to aged beer at bottling to induce fermentation (bottle conditioning).

priming sugar. A small amount of corn, malt, or cane sugar added to bulk beer prior to racking or at bottling to induce a new fermentation and create carbonation.

racking. The process of transferring beer from one container to another, especially into the final package (bottles, kegs, and so on).

reagent. A substance involved in a reaction that identifies the strength of the substance being measured.

real ale. A name for draught (or bottled) beer brewed from the traditional ingredients, matured by secondary fermentation in the container from which it is dispensed, and served without the use of extraneous carbon dioxide. Real ale is found primarily in Britain, where it has been championed by the consumer rights group called the Campaign for Real Ale (CAMRA).

recirculation. *See* vorlauf.

resin. Noncrystalline (amorphous) plant excretions.

rest. Mash rest. Holding the mash at a specific temperature to induce certain enzymatic changes.

ropy fermentation. Viscous gelatinous blobs, or "rope," from bacterial contamination.

rousing. Creating turbulence by agitation. Mixing.

runnings. The wort or sweet liquid that is collected during the lautering of the wet mash.

saccharification. The naturally occurring process in which malt starch is converted into fermentable sugars, primarily maltose. Also called mashing, since saccharification occurs during the mash rest.

saccharometer. An instrument that determines the sugar concentration of a solution by measuring the specific gravity.

secondary fermentation. 1. The second, slower stage of fermentation, which, depending on the type of beer, lasts from a few weeks to many months. 2. A fermentation occurring in bottles or casks that is initiated by priming or by adding yeast.

sparge. The even distribution or spray of hot water over the saccharified mash to rinse free the extract from the grist.

sparging. Spraying the spent grains in the mash with hot water to retrieve the remaining malt sugar. This is done at the end of the mashing (saccharification) process.

specific gravity (SG). A measure of a substance's density as compared to that of water, which is given the value of 1.000 at 39.2 °F (4 °C). Specific gravity has no accompanying units because it is expressed as a ratio. Specific gravity is the density of a solution in grams per milliliter.

Standard Reference Method (SRM) and **European Brewery Convention (EBC).** Two different analytical methods of describing color developed by comparing color samples. Degrees SRM, approximately equivalent to degrees Lovibond, are used by the ASBC (American Society of Brewing Chemists), while degrees EBC are European units. The following equations show approximate conversions: (EBC) = 2.65 × (SRM) − 1.2; SRM = 0.377 × (EBC) + 0.46.

starch. A polymer of sugar molecules. The chief form of energy storage for most plants. It is from starch that the relevant sugars for brewing are derived.

starter. A batch of fermenting yeast added to the wort to initiate fermentation.

Steele's masher. A device used in many traditional British independent breweries to hydrate the grain as it is added to the mash tun. It consists of an archemedian screw and a metal housing.

steeping. The initial processing step in malting in which the raw barley is soaked in water and periodically aerated to induce germination.

strike temperature. The initial (target) temperature of the water when the malted barley is added to it to create the mash.

swirl tank. *See* whirlpool.

tannin. Astringent polyphenolic compounds, capable of colliding with proteins and either precipitating or forming haze fractions. Oxidized polyphenols form color compounds relevant in beer. *See also* polyphenol.

terminal extract. The density of the fully fermented beer.

titration. Measurement of a substance in solution by the addition of a standard disclosing solution to initiate an indicative color change.

trisaccharide. A sugar composed of three monosaccharides joined by the removal of water molecules.

trub. Flocks of haze-forming particles resulting from the precipitation of proteins, hop oils, and tannins during the boiling and cooling stages of brewing.

turbidity. Sediment in suspension. Hazy, murky.

ullage. The empty space between a liquid and the top of its container. Also called airspace or headspace.

utensils. Arcane word meaning brewery equipment.

viscosity. The resistance of a fluid to flow.

volatile. Readily vaporized, especially esters, essential oils, and higher alcohols.

volume of beer. To calculate the approximate volumetric alcohol content, subtract the terminal gravity from the original gravity and divide the result by 75. For example: $1.050 - 1.012 = 0.038 / 0.75 = 0.05$ or 5% ABV.

vorlauf. The practice of running the sweet wort back through the bed of grain to filter out the finest particles and return a clear wort to the kettle.

water hardness. The degree of dissolved minerals in water. Usually expressed in parts per million (ppm) or grains per gallon (gpg).

whirlpool. A brewhouse vessel designed to create a vortex in the hopped wort after the boil to help coagulate the precipitated trub for a clean racking into the primary fermenter.

wort. Mash extract (sweet wort). The hopped sugar solution before pitching, before it is fermented into beer.

Yorkshire stone squares. A once-popular fermentation method in the Northeast of England characterized by slate construction, the necessity of manual rousing, and use of a highly flocculant yeast. Now only used in a very few breweries in Yorkshire and surrounding counties.

Index

Abel Brown's, mild ale by, 207

Adjuncts, 77-78, 174, 229; coloring, 84-85; copper, 78, 82-84; grain, 79; mash tun, 78-79

Adnam's, mild ale by, 173, 207

Adnam's Old Ale, OG of, 63

Aeration, 130, 229; hot-side, 139-40

Age, classification by, 24

Aging, 48, 76

AK, 229; meaning of, 58-59; recipe for, 201

Albumin, 108, 229

Ale conners/konners, 58

Ale kyte, 58, 186

Ales, 37, 230; cask ale and, 155-56; meaning of, 35, 36; roots of, 12; unhopped, 35

Alibi Red Mild, 198; recipe for, 203

Alkalis, cleaning with, 146, 158

All-grain, 197, 230

Alpha acids, 134, 148, 230; total, 136

Amber malt, medium-roasted, 75

American Handy-Book of Brewing, Malting and Auxiliary Trades, 43-44

American Tettnanger, 91

Amsinck, George Stewart, 25-26, 126; on fermentation, 94; on grinding, 122; on hops, 86; on Kents, 87; on pitching, 141; on rousing, 104

Anise, experimenting with, 25

Ansells, mild ale by, 176, 208

Antique beers, brewing, 147-50

Aroma, 74, 153; of hops, 137, 138, 148, 156; mild ale, 57, 59-63; oxidized, 140; roast and, 74; undesirable, 132

Art of Brewing, on mild ales/ gravity, 41

Asquith, Herbert, 58

Attemperators, 112, 142 (photo), 144, 231

Attenuation, 116, 144, 231

Bacteria, 48, 76, 124; problems with, 17, 147

Bain, Neil: Highgate Dark and, 178

Index

Index

Index

Maturation, 107; extended, 118

McGuiness, mild ale by, 213

McMullen and Sons Ltd., AK by, 185-87

McMullen's Brewery, 58, 60-61, 186 (photo), 191; mild ale by, 213

McMullen's Original AK, 50, 52, 58, 61, 185-87; color/clarity of, 53-54; OG of, 63

Measurement conversions, list of, 223

Meaux's Horse Shoe Brewery, 43; vat at, 32

Melanoidins, 15, 241

Merrie Monk, 62, 180

Mesh-bottomed dishes, 124

Microflora, fermentation and, 20

Microorganisms, 145; alcoholic content and, 20; culturing, 142

Mild, 12, 37, 242; bitter and, 85; as class of beer, 23-24; meaning of, 36

Mild Ale, c. 1824, recipe for, 206

Mild ales: accessibility of, 40; bitters and, 46; brewing, 5, 7-8, 98; brown ales and, 45, 56; commercially produced, 173-95, 197; cousins of, 27-30; decline of, 49, 63;

defining, 51, 56-57; development of, 4, 8-9, 21, 30, 37-43; in early popular literature, 22-23; English ingredients for, 65; formulations analysis of, 175 (table); future for, 47-50; gravity of, 36, 41, 42, 47; hopping of, 41; ingredients of, 65-96, 174; modern, 8, 43-47, 55; OG of, 53; pales and, 36, 46; popularity of, 9, 11, 33, 43, 46-47; porters and, 39; profiles of, 51-63, 54 (table); roles for, 7-8; roots of, 1, 11-12; subcategories of, 51

Mild beers, brown beers and, 44-45

Mill, described, 99-100

Mitchell and Butlers, mild ale by, 214

Mitchell's, mild ale by, 213

Modification, 123, 242

Molasses, 82, 83, 163, 164

Molson Breweries, whirlpool tank by, 140

Moorehouses, mild ale by, 214

Morrell's, mild ale by, 214

Munich lager strain, 95

Muntons malt, 69

Index

Pedigree Bitter, 93, 110

Pembroke, mild ale by, 214

Perfect Pint: Producing Real Ale in America, The (Daniels), 168

Perforated carbonation/aeration stone, 170

Perkins, mild ale by, 39

Perry, Guy, 184

Pewter tankards, 97, 171

pH, 243; fermentation and, 134

Phil's Lauter, 198

Phoenix, mild ale by, 214

Phosphates, 132, 243

Pipkin malt, 68

Pitching, 116, 141, 244; temperatures at, 144

Pitching rates, 163; average, 143 (table)

Pliny the Younger, on *curmi,* 12

Plumage Archer malt, 68

PMD Mild, 191-94

Polysaccharides, 132, 244

Porter (brewer), mild ale by, 214

Porters, 7, 8, 76; bitters and, 46; brewing, 2, 30; brown malt for, 34; classification of, 36-37; consumption of, 39; decline of, 38, 39, 40; development of, 21, 28-30, 34; gravity of, 41; mild ale and, 5, 27-30, 39; naming, 28; pales and, 38, 46; quest for, 1, 5; stouts and, 24; vatted, 40

Porter vats, 31 (illus.)

Practical Brewings: A Series of Fifty Brewings (Amsinck), quote from, 86, 87, 94, 104, 122, 126, 141

Precipitation, 135, 244

Present-use ales, flavor of, 21

Primary fermentation, 107, 111, 151, 156, 162, 245; described, 143-45; sugar and, 160; temperature for, 198

Priming, 163, 245

Priming sugar, 160-64, 245; determining dosages of, 169; mixing, 165

Private Brewer's Guide, on brown beer/porter, 26

Protein haze, 55, 165

Protz, Roger: mild ales and, 4

Pubs, growth of, 38

Racking, 154, 154 (photo), 159, 162, 245; described, 164-66; finings and, 160; temperature at, 145

Rainer Brewing Company, cylindro-conical fermentation and, 117

About the Author

David Sutula could not stand the taste of beer until his junior year in college when he and a friend took a trip to Portland, Maine. While there, they stumbled upon Gritty McDuff's Brewery, where David requested the most appetizing-sounding item on the menu—a stout. Two weeks later, David was at home and bottling his first homebrew.

David has worked professionally in the Cleveland brewing industry since 1993. Currently, he is the head brewer at the Quarry Ridge Brewery in Berea, Ohio. When he is not driving the horse-drawn beer dray to make deliveries around historic Berea, David is perched atop the brew house making traditional British ales, continental lagers, and indigenous American beers.